Daily Observations
Thoreau on the Days of the Year

D1566141

Daily Observations

THOREAU ON THE DAYS OF THE YEAR

Edited by Steve Grant

Engravings by Barry Moser

UNIVERSITY OF MASSACHUSETTS PRESS

AMHERST & BOSTON

Published in cooperation with

THE THOREAU SOCIETY

LC 2005005406
ISBN 1-55849-501-0 (library cloth ed.); 500-2 (paper)

Set in Monotype Bell
Printed on recycled paper by Thomson-Shore, Inc.

Library of Congress Cataloging-in-Publication Data

Thoreau, Henry David, 1817–1862.
Daily observations : Thoreau on the days of the year / edited by Steve Grant.
p. cm. — (The spirit of Thoreau series)
Includes bibliographical references.
ISBN 1-55849-500-2 (pbk. : alk. paper) —
ISBN 1-55849-501-0 (library cloth : alk. paper)
1. Thoreau, Henry David, 1817–1862—Quotations.
2. Quotations, American. 3. Literary calendars.
I. Title: Thoreau on the days of the year. II. Grant, Steve, 1946– III. Title.
PS3042.G73 2005
818'.309—dc22
2005005406

British Library Cataloguing in Publication data are available.

INTRODUCTION
Henry David Thoreau and His Journal
STEVE GRANT

THIS BOOK is drawn entirely from the pages of Henry David Thoreau's *Journal*. It is organized as a daybook, with a journal excerpt for each day of the year, usually but a fraction of what Thoreau entered for that day. It constitutes a circle of the seasons, which Thoreau watched intensely and wrote about almost daily. There is much else here, too, because Thoreau always kept one eye on society—and its shortcomings.

To those unfamiliar with his life, Henry David Thoreau is often regarded as the hermit who lived in a little hut in the woods beside Walden Pond and wrote a book. This Thoreau was antisocial, a scold, and a misfit. He *could* be difficult. He *did* live by himself at Walden Pond for twenty-six months. He *did* spend much of a Thanksgiving Day alone in a swamp. But the real Thoreau was affirmative as well, humanitarian and far more nuanced. He had friends, lifelong friends with whom he spent countless hours. He was close to his family, and he interacted all his life with the Concord community, albeit in his uncompromising and sometimes off-putting way. Even at Walden he had frequent visitors. "If I have no friend, what is Nature to me?" he once wrote. One prominent Thoreau scholar, Robert D. Richardson Jr., has called him a semidomesticated recluse. That seems fair.

Walden, the masterpiece that grew from his experience at the pond, is well known. But Thoreau left a substantial body of other literature as well, including some classic essays. Thoreau scholars in the process of producing the definitive texts of his writings expect them to run to thirty volumes. Among other works already available are *Cape Cod*, a travel narrative that is a pleasant read even today and perhaps the most accessible of Thoreau's writings, and his first book, *A Week on the Concord and Merrimack Rivers*, which newcomers to Thoreau sometimes find less engaging.

Behind all of these works is his *Journal*, which he kept for twenty-four years. Thoreau used it extensively in producing his lectures, essays, and books, including *Walden*, sometimes actually tearing pages from the journal as he worked. The *Journal* can be considered a rough-draft of his best-known lectures and books, then, but to call it that is nonetheless unfair; it is too good, too polished, and too rich a mine of material to be approached as an unfinished work. The *Journal* is a magnificent achievement in its own right. To read Thoreau's *Journal* is to be drawn intimately into the subtle changes in nature that are the daily manifestations of the ever-changing seasons. Thoreau's philosophy of a simple life unfettered by possessions flows through the *Journal*, peppered with his thoughts on subjects as varied as slavery, clothing fashions, politics, and the proper diet. It is diary, it is social commentary, it is fundamental natural history. It is where you will find the Henry David Thoreau who took children berry picking, the Thoreau who became *the* last word in Concord on any natural history question. "For the connoisseur," wrote Walter R. Harding, a Thoreau biographer and lifelong student of his work, "it is the best of Thoreau."

The necessary biographical facts are these: Thoreau was born on 12 July 1817 in Concord, Massachusetts, then a town of two thousand people about twenty miles northwest of Boston. It was an agricultural town, with much of the land already cleared for farming. He was educated at Harvard, was a skilled surveyor, and sometimes helped his father with the family pencil company. He fell in love and proposed marriage to Ellen Sewall, a pretty young woman whose father disapproved of Thoreau's Transcendentalist views. She declined; he never married. Most days he read and wrote in the morning, walked or went boating in the afternoon. He loved blueberries and crickets and sunsets. He loved paradox, too, and, like the rest of us, he was contradictory at times. One day he might be romanticizing the life of the farmer, the next complaining that all a farmer did was work.

He was a fervent abolitionist whose home was part of the Underground Railroad helping runaway slaves to freedom. He was an ecologist before the term was ever coined, and was thought to have been writing a natural history of Concord when he died. Virtually every nature writer of consequence since has consciously or unconsciously bowed to his influence.

Thoreau began his journal on 22 October 1837, after Ralph Waldo Emerson asked if he kept one. It continued until 3 November 1861, only months before he died of tuberculosis on 6 May 1862, short of his forty-fifth birthday. Practically every theme that Thoreau tackled, every idea, every perceptive observation can be found first in the journal. Because Thoreau was a careful and perceptive observer of nature and society, the journal entries are invaluable today for what they can tell us about mid-nineteenth-century life. They also constitute an inventory of plant and animal life in Concord for the period, itself priceless.

Comparatively few people read the *Journal*, however, and one reason has to be its size, nearly two million words. The text now being edited is expected to total sixteen volumes. It can be slow-going in places, as when Thoreau as a young man lays down quotations from his reading or in later years gives us exhaustive descriptions of Walden Pond water temperatures. But far more often the reader is rewarded with anecdote and observation in prose that is always sturdy, often lyrical, and sometimes as good as anything he ever wrote.

Included in this collection are Thoreau's observations on the art of writing, the value of communes, the need for wilderness. There are anecdotes, including Thoreau's role in secreting a slave though Concord one day. And there is plain, descriptive writing, much of it on nature. A sense of nineteenth-century life emerges; Thoreau from his boat hears a man singing on a nearby road, a song that likely would be overwhelmed by the din of auto traffic today. On a cool spring morning he tells us that a few slats of wood are sufficient to take the chill from his chamber.

Through it all is the Thoreau philosophy, sometimes summed up in those three famous words from *Walden*, "simplicity, simplicity, simplicity!"

What we don't find in the *Journal* is much of a deeply personal nature. Thoreau never tells us explicitly what the loss of Ellen Sewell meant to him, for example, and he was often stingy or circumspect in providing details about his relations with others. There are occasionally revealing glimpses of his family life, however, as when Thoreau describes a bitter cold night with the family in front of the fireplace, or, another day, relates this incident: "My Aunt Maria asked me to read the life of Dr. Chalmers, which however I did not promise to do. Yesterday, Sunday, she was heard through the partition shouting to my Aunt Jane, who is deaf, 'Think of it! He stood half an hour to-day to hear the frogs croak, and he wouldn't read the life of Chalmers.'"

❦   ❦   ❦

This collection traces its origins to a daily memo I began distributing to several close friends at the *Hartford Courant* more than a decade ago. As I slowly worked my way through the Journal—perhaps five or ten pages a day—I selected quotations and sent them to my friends by e-mail. Soon, others asked to receive these passages, and now, long after I have completed a first reading of the *Journal*, several dozen people receive them. The unsolicited comments I get back are often spirited, sometimes applauding Thoreau's perspective, sometimes questioning it, sometimes denouncing it. I take this as emphatic evidence of Thoreau's relevance. He still makes us think. He elicits a response.

In selecting passages for this daybook I have in many instances chosen a brief passage that seemed to capture the essence of a longer journal entry. I tried to do so with sensitivity. Many of these quotations are aphoristic and it is tempting to hype them as Thoreauvian "sound bites," nineteenth-century versions of today's made-for-TV one-liners. I'll resist the temptation because they are two completely different things. Few, if any, of today's sound bites will stand the test of time, but these do, as when Thoreau pronounces on a spring day: "You must taste the first glass of the day's nectar, if you would get all the spirit of it."

Thoreau is astonishingly modern, which no doubt helps explain his growing appeal, and why my colleagues find fragments of his journal fascinating and provocative. His views on Native Americans anticipated those often voiced today. He understood their intimacy with nature and sought to learn from them. He was outraged by slavery. He was among the first to insist that America protect some of its wildest lands for future generations.

On a New Year's Day, at age thirty-four, Thoreau wrote in his journal, "I wish to be translated to the future—& look at my work as it were at a structure on the plain, to observe what portions have crumbled under the influence of the elements." Remarkably little has crumbled. If anything, Thoreau's message that we ought to strive for a simple and honest life seems more timely as the years go by—if ever harder to attain. This from 11 January 1852: "We sometimes find ourselves living fast—unprofitably & coarsely even—as we catch ourselves eating our meals in unaccountable haste—But in one sense we cannot live too leisurely—Let me not live as if time was short. Catch the pace of the seasons—have leisure to attend to every phenomenon of nature—and to entertain every thought that comes to you. Let your life be a leisurely progress through the realms of nature."

At Thoreau's funeral service, Ralph Waldo Emerson observed, "The country knows not yet, or in the least part, how great a son it has lost."

It took time, but the country and the world eventually realized what it had lost. All of his works are either in print—often there are many editions to choose from—or will be in print shortly. There are Internet chat sites devoted to Thoreau, and *Walden* has been translated into many languages. His influence today extends far beyond what it was when he died. In the increasingly popular nature and literature courses offered in America's colleges and universities, Thoreau is a constant, almost certainly the most assigned writer in the long tradition of the genre.

Part of the joy in reading the *Journal* is discovering passages that speak to you, ideas or thoughts that, as Thoreau wrote, "we already half know." It is testament to the high quality of the journal that for many days of the year it was difficult choosing among the observations, pronouncements, and anecdotes available. Perhaps you will find some favorites of your own here, and one day turn to the *Journal* itself, where you will discover many more.

DAILY OBSERVATIONS
Thoreau on the Days of the Year

JANUARY

1 January 1852 ❧ I HAVE SO MUCH FAITH in the power of truth to communicate itself, that I should not believe a friend if he should tell me that he had given credit to an unjust rumor concerning me.

2 January 1859 ❧ WHEN I HEAR the hypercritical quarrelling about grammar and style, the position of the particles, etc. etc., stretching or contracting every speaker to certain rules of theirs,—Mr. Webster, perhaps, not having spoken according to Mr. Kirkham's rule,—I see that they forget that the first requisite and rule is that expression shall be vital and natural, as much as the voice of a brute or an interjection: first of all, mother tongue; and last of all, artificial or father tongue. Essentially your truest poetic sentence is as free and lawless as a lamb's bleat. The grammarian is often one who can neither cry nor laugh, yet thinks that he can express human emotions. So the posture-masters tell you how you shall walk,—turning your toes out, perhaps excessively,—but so the beautiful walkers are not made.

3 January 1853 ❧ I HAVE A ROOM all to my self; it is Nature It is a place beyond the jurisdiction of human governments. Pile up your books the records of sadness—your saws & your laws— Nature is glad outside-& her merry worms within will erelong topple them down.

4 January 1857 ❦ AFTER SPENDING four or five days surveying and drawing a plan incessantly, I especially feel the necessity of putting myself in communication with nature again, to recover my tone, to withdraw out of the wearying and unprofitable world of affairs. The things I have been doing have but a fleeting and accidental importance, however much men are immersed in them, and yield very little valuable fruit. I would fain have been wading through the woods and fields and conversing with the sane snow. Having waded in the very shallowest stream of time, I would now bathe my temples in eternity. I wish again to participate in the serenity of nature, to share the happiness of the river and the woods.

5 January 1860 ❦ A MAN RECEIVES only what he is ready to receive, whether physically or intellectually or morally, as animals conceive at certain seasons their kind only. We hear and apprehend only what we already half know. If there is something which does not concern me, which is out of my line, which by experience or by genius my attention is not drawn to, however novel and remarkable it may be, if it is spoken, we hear it not, if it is written, we read it not, or if we read it, it does not detain us. Every man thus *tracks himself* through life, in all his hearing and reading and observation and travelling.

6 January 1858 ❦ . . . MY ATTENTION was caught by a snowflake on my coat-sleeve. It was one of those perfect, crystalline, star-shaped ones, six-rayed, like a flat wheel with six spokes, only the spokes were perfect little pine trees in shape, arranged around a central spangle. This little object, which, with many of its fellows, rested unmelting on my coat, so perfect and beautiful, reminded me that Nature had not lost her pristine vigor yet, and why should man lose heart?

7 January 1852 ❧ WE NEVER TIRE of the drama of sunset. I go forth each afternoon & look into the west ¼ of an hour before sunset with fresh curiosity to see what new picture will be painted there—what new panorama exhibited—what new dissolving views—can Washington Street or Broad-Way show anything as good? Every day a new picture is painted and framed, held up for half an hour—in such lights as the great artist chooses & then with drawn—& the curtain falls.

8 January 1854 ❧ THE MORNING HOPE is soon lost in what becomes the routine of the day, and we do not recover ourselves again until we land on the pensive shores of evening, shores which skirt the great western continent of the night.

9 January 1855 ❧ WHAT A STRONG and hearty but reckless, hit-or-miss style had some of the early writers of New England, like Josselyn and William Wood and others elsewhere in those days; as if they spoke with a relish, smacking their lips like a coach whip, caring more to speak heartily than scientifically true. They are not to be caught napping by the wonders of Nature in a new country, and perhaps are often more ready to appreciate them than she is to exhibit them. They give you one piece of nature, at any rate, and that is themselves. (Cotton Mather, too, has a rich phrase.) They use a strong, coarse, homely speech which cannot always be found in the dictionary, nor sometimes be heard in polite society, but which brings you very near to the thing itself described. The strong new soil speaks through them.

10 January 1856 ❧ THE KITCHEN WINDOWS were magnificent last night, with their frost sheaves, surpassing any cut or ground glass.

11 January 1852 ❦ LET ME NOT LIVE as if time was short. Catch the pace of the seasons—have leisure to attend to every phenomenon of nature—and to entertain every thought that comes to you. Let your life be a leisurely progress through the realms of nature.

12 January 1855 ❦ PERHAPS WHAT MOST moves us in winter is some reminiscence of far-off summer. How we leap by the side of the open brooks! What beauty in the running brooks! What life! What society! The cold is merely superficial; it is summer still at the core, far, far within. It is in the cawing of the crow, the crowing of the cock, the warmth of the sun on our backs.

13 January 1856 ❦ IN OUR WORKSHOPS we pride ourselves on discovering a use for what had previously been regarded as waste, but how partial and accidental our economy compared with Nature's. In Nature nothing is wasted.

14 January 1854 ❦ I JUST HAD A COAT come home from the tailor's. Ah me! Who am I that should wear this coat? It was fitted upon one of the devil's angels about my size. Of what use that measuring of me if he did not measure my character, but only the breadth of my shoulders, as it were a peg to hang it on. This is not the figure that I cut. This is the figure the tailor cuts. That presumptuous and impertinent fashion whispered in his ear, so that he heard no word of mine. As if I had said, "Not my will, O Fashion, but thine be done."

15 January 1857 ❦ But let us hear a strain of music, we are at once advertised of a life which no man had told us of, which no preacher preaches. Suppose I try to describe faithfully the prospect which a strain of music exhibits to me. The field of my life becomes a boundless plain, glorious to tread, with no death nor disappointment at the end of it. All meanness and trivialness disappear. I become adequate to any deed. No particulars survive this expansion; persons do not survive it. In the light of this strain there is no thou nor I. We are actually lifted above ourselves.

16 January 1852 ❦ I see that to some men their relation to mankind is all important It is fatal in their eyes to outrage the opinions and customs of their fellow men. Failure and success are therefore never proved by them by absolute and universal tests. I feel myself not so vitally related to my fellow men.

17 January 1852 ❦ In proportion as I have celestial thoughts, is the necessity for me to be out and behold the western sky before sunset these winter days. That is the symbol of the unclouded mind that knows neither winter nor summer. What is your thought like? That is the hue—that the purity & transparency and distance from earthly taint of my inmost mind—for whatever we see without is a symbol of something within—& that which is farthest off—is the symbol of what is deepest within. The lover of contemplation accordingly will gaze much into the sky.— Fair thoughts & a serene mind make fair days.

18 January 1856 ❦ THIS IS A VERY MILD, melting winter day, but clear and bright, yet I see the blue shadows on the snow at Walden. The snow lies very level there, about ten inches deep, and for the most part bears me as I go across with my hatchet. I think I never saw a more elysian blue than my shadow. I am turned into a tall blue Persian from my cap to my boots, such as no mortal dye can produce, with an amethystine hatchet in my hand. I am in raptures at my own shadow. What if the substance were of as ethereal a nature?

19 January 1841 ❦ I ANTICIPATE a more thorough sympathy with nature when my thigh-bones shall strew the ground like the boughs which the wind has scattered.— These troublesome humors will flower into early anemonies, and perhaps in the very lachrymal sinus, nourished by its juices, some young pine or oak will strike root.

20 January 1856 ❦ IN MY EXPERIENCE I have found nothing so truly impoverishing as what is called wealth, *i. e.* the command of greater means than you had before possessed, though comparatively few and slight still, for you thus inevitably acquire a more expensive habit of living, and even the very same necessaries and comforts cost you more than they once did.

21 January 1852 ❦ A MAN DOES BEST when he is most himself.

22 January 1852 ❦ EACH THOUGHT THAT is welcomed and recorded is a nest egg—by the side of which more will be laid. Thoughts accidentally thrown together become a frame—in which more may be developed-& exhibited. Perhaps this is the main value of a habit of writing—of keeping a journal. That so we remember our best hours—& stimulate ourselves. My thoughts are my company— They have a certain individuality & separate existence—aye personality. Having by chance recorded a few disconnected thoughts and then brought them into juxtaposition—they suggest a whole new field in which it was possible to labor & to think. Thought begat thought.

23 January 1858 ❦ To INSURE HEALTH, a man's relation to Nature must come very near to a personal one; he must be conscious of a friendliness in her; when human friends fail or die, she must stand in the gap to him. I cannot conceive of any life which deserves the name, unless there is a certain tender relation to Nature. This it is which makes winter warm, and supplies society in the desert and wilderness. Unless Nature sympathizes with and speaks to us, as it were, the most fertile and blooming regions are barren and dreary.

24 January 1852 ❦ IF THOU ART A WRITER write as if thy time was short—for it is indeed short at the longest. Improve each occasion when thy soul is reached—drain the cup of inspiration to its last dregs—fear no intemperance in that. for the years will come when otherwise thou wilt regret opportunities unimproved. The spring will not last forever. These fertile & expanding seasons of thy life—when the rain reaches thy root—when thy vigor shoots when thy flower is budding—shall be fewer & farther between.

25 January 1858 ❦ YOU MUST LOVE the crust of the earth on which you dwell more than the sweet crust of any bread or cake. You must be able to extract nutriment out of a sandheap. You must have so good an appetite as this, else you will live in vain.

26 January 1853 ❧ Now I go a fishing & a hunting every day but omit the fish & the game—which are the least important part— I have learned to do without them. They were indispensable only as long as I was a boy—

27 January 1855 ❧ New England is flooded with the "Official Schemes of the Maryland State Lotteries," and in this that State is no less unprincipled than in her slaveholding. Maryland, and every fool who buys a ticket of her, is bound straight to the bottomless pit. The state of Maryland is a moral fungus.

28 January 1852 ❧ If you mean by hard times—times not when there is no bread, but when there is no cake, I have no sympathy with you.

29 January 1852 ❧ I am often reminded that if I had bestowed on me the wealth of Croesus, my aims must still be the same & my means essentially the same.

30 January 1854 ❧ I will be a countryman. I will not go to the city, even in winter, any more than the sallows and sweetgale by the river do.

31 January 1854 ❧ We too have our thaws. They come to our January moods, when our ice cracks, and our sluices break loose. Thought that was frozen up under stern experience gushes forth in feeling and expression.

FEBRUARY

1 February 1852 ❦ I T DEPENDS upon how a man has spent his day—whether he has any right to be in his bed. So spend some hours that you may have a right to sleep in the sunshine.

2 February 1854 ❦ A LREADY we begin to anticipate spring, and this is an important difference between this time and a month ago. We begin to say that the day is springlike.

Is not January the hardest month to get through? When you have weathered that, you get into the gulfstream of winter, nearer the shores of spring.

3 February 1852 ❦ T HOSE WHO HAVE expressed the purest & deepest love of nature—have not recorded it on the bark of the trees with the lichens—they have left no momento of it there—but if I would read their books I must go to the city—so strange & repulsive both to them & to me—& deal with men & institutions with whom I have no sympathy. When I have just been there on this errand, it seems too great a price to pay, for access even to the works of Homer or Chaucer—or Linnaeus.

4 February 1857 ❦ I SEE THAT the infidels and skeptics have formed themselves into churches and weekly gather together at the ringing of a bell.

5 February 1860 ❦ Coming home last night in the twilight, I recognized a neighbor a dozen rods off by his walk or carriage, though it was so dark that I could not see a single feature of his person. Indeed, his person was all covered up excepting his face and hands, and I could not possibly have distinguished these at this distance from another man's. Nor was it owing to any peculiarity in his dress, for I should have known him though he had had on a perfectly new suit. It was because the man within the clothes moved them in a peculiar manner that I knew him thus at once at a distance and in the twilight. He made a certain figure in any clothes he might wear, and moved in it in a peculiar manner. Indeed, we have a very intimate knowledge of one another; we see through thick and thin; spirit meets spirit. A man hangs out innumerable signs by which we may know him.

6 February 1841 ❦ I feel slightly complimented when nature condescends to make use of me without my knowledge—as when I help scatter her seeds in my walk—or carry burs and cockles on my clothes from field to field—

7 February 1855 ❦ The coldest night for a long, long time was last. Sheets froze stiff about the faces. Cat mewed to have the door opened, but was at first disinclined to go out. When she came in at nine she smelt of meadow-hay. We all took her up and smelled of her, it was so fragrant. Had cuddled in some barn. People dreaded to go to bed. The ground cracked in the night as if a powder-mill had blown up, and the timbers of the house also. My pail of water was frozen in the morning so that I could not break it. Must leave many buttons unbuttoned, owing to numb fingers. Iron was like fire in the hands. Thermometer at about 7:30 A.M. gone into the bulb, -19° at least. The cold has stopped the clock. Every bearded man in the street is a graybeard. Bread, meat, milk, cheese, etc., etc., all frozen. See the inside of your cellar door all covered and sparkling with frost like Golconda. Pity the poor who have not a large wood-pile. The latches are white with frost, and every nail-head in entries, etc., has a white cap.

8 February 1852 ❦ WHAT IF THERE IS less fire on the hearth, if there is more in the heart.

9 February 1852 ❦ WHEN I BREAK OFF a twig of green-barked sassafras as I am going through the woods now—& smell it, I am startled to find it fragrant as in summer— It is an importation of all the spices of oriental summers into our New England winter.

10 February 1841 ❦ LET OUR WORDS be such as we may un-blushingly behold sculptured in granite on the walls—to the least syllable.

11 February 1853 ❦ I AM SURPRISED that we make no more ado about echoes— They are almost the only kindred voices that I hear.

12 February 1851 ❦ I TRUST THAT the walkers of the present day are conscious of the blessings which they enjoy in the comparative freedom with which they can ramble over the country & enjoy the landscape—anticipating with compassion that future day when possibly it will be partitioned off into so called pleasure grounds where only a few may enjoy the narrow & exclusive pleasure which is compatible with ownership. When walking over the surface of Gods earth—shall be construed to mean trespassing on some gentleman's grounds. When fences shall be multiplied & man traps & other engines invented to confine men to the public road. I am thankfull that we have yet so much room in America.

13 February 1859 ❦ THE OLD ICE is covered with a dry, powdery snow about one inch deep, from which, as I walk toward the sun, this perfectly clear, bright afternoon, at 3:30 o'clock, the colors of the rainbow are reflected from a myriad fine facets. It is as if the dust of diamonds and other precious stones were spread all around.

14 February 1851 ❦ WE LEARN by the January thaw that the winter is intermittent and are reminded of other seasons— The back of the winter is broken

15 February 1859 ❦ AGAINST BITTERN CLIFF I feel the first drop strike the right slope of my nose and run down the ravine there. Such is the origin of rivers.

16 February 1859 ❦ THE HEN HAWK and the pine are friends. The same thing which keeps the hen-hawk in the woods, away from the cities, keeps me here. That bird settles with confidence on a white pine top and not upon your weathercock. That bird will not be poultry of yours, lays no eggs for you, forever hides its nest. Though willed, or *wild*, it is not willful in its wildness. The unsympathizing man regards the wildness of some animals, their strangeness to him, as a sin; as if all their virtue consisted in their tamableness. He has always a charge in his gun ready for their extermination. What we call wildness is a civilization other than our own. The hen-hawk shuns the farmer, but it seeks the friendly shelter and support of the pine. It will not consent to walk in the barn-yard, but it loves to soar above the clouds. It has its own way and is beautiful, when we would fain subject it to our will. So any surpassing work of art is strange and wild to the mass of men, as is genius itself.

17 February 1841 ❦ WOULD IT NOT BE WELL for us to consider if our deed will warrant the expense of nature. Will it maintain the sun's light?

18 February 1860 ❦ I FEEL, OF COURSE, very ignorant in a museum. I know nothing about the things which they have there,—no more than I should know my friends in the tomb. I walk amid those jars of bloated creatures which they label frogs, a total stranger, without the least froggy thought being suggested. Not one of them can croak. They leave behind all life they that enter there, both frogs and men.

19 February 1855 ❧ MANY WILL COMPLAIN of my lectures that they are transcendental. "Can't understand them." "Would you have us return to the savage state?" etc., etc. A criticism true enough, it may be, from their point of view. But the fact is, the earnest lecturer can speak only to his like, and the adapting of himself to his audience is a mere compliment which he pays them. If you wish to know how I think, you must endeavor to put yourself in my place. If you wish me to speak as if I were you, that is another affair.

20 February 1859 ❧ IN THE COMPOSITION it is the greatest art to find out as quickly as possible which are the best passages you have written, and tear the rest away to come at them. Even the poorest parts will be most effective when they serve these, as pediments to the column.

21 February 1854 ❧ YOU CANNOT WALK too early in new fallen snow—to get the sense of purity novelty & unexploredness.

22 February 1841 ❧ WE SHOULD MAKE our notch every day on our characters as Robinson Crusoe on his stick. We must be at the helm at least once a day—we must feel the tiller rope in our hands, and know that if we sail, we steer.

23 February 1841 ❧ THE CARE OF THE BODY is the highest exercise of prudence.

24 February 1852 ❧ AS WE GROW OLDER—is it not ominous that we have more to write about evening—less about morning.

25 February 1859 ❦ MEASURE YOUR HEALTH by your sympathy with morning and spring. If there is no response in you to the awakening of nature,—if the prospect of an early morning walk does not banish sleep, if the warble of the first bluebird does not thrill you,—know that the morning and spring of your life are past. Thus may you feel your pulse.

26 February 1852 ❦ WE ARE TOLD TODAY that civilization is making rapid progress—the tendency is ever upward—substantial justice is done even by human courts— You may trust the good intentions of mankind.— We read to-morrow in the newspapers that the French nation is on the eve of going to war with England to give employment to her army.

27 February 1860 ❦ I WALK DOWN the river below Flint's on the north side. The sudden apparition of this dark-blue water on the surface of the earth is exciting. I must now walk where I can see the most water, as to the most living part of nature. This is the blood of the earth, and we see its blue arteries pulsing with new life now.

28 February 1856 ❦ OUR YOUNG maltese cat Min, which has been absent five cold nights, the ground covered deep with crusted snow,—her first absence,—and given up for dead, has at length returned at daylight, awakening the whole house with her mewing and afraid of the strange girl we have got in the meanwhile. She is a mere wrack of skin and bones, with a sharp nose and wiry tail. She is as one returned from the dead. There is as much rejoicing as at the return of the prodigal son, and if we had a fatted calf we should kill it. Various are the conjectures as to her adventures,—whether she has had a fit, been shut up somewhere, or lost, torn in pieces by a certain terrier or frozen to death. In the meanwhile she is fed with the best that the house affords, minced meats and saucers of warmed milk, and, with the aid of unstinted sleep in all laps in succession, is fast picking up her crumbs. She has already found her old place under the stove, and is preparing to make a stew of her brains there.

29 February 1852 ❦ FOR THE PAST MONTH there has been more sea-room in the day—without so great danger of running a ground on one of those two promontories that make it arduous to navigate the winter day—the morning or the evening. It is a narrow pass—& you must go through with the tide. Might not some of my pages be called —The short days of Winter?

MARCH

1 March 1852 ❦ AFTER HAVING READ various books on various subjects for some months I take up "a report on "Farms by a committee of Middlesex Husbandmen—and read of the number of acres of bog that some farmer has redeemed & the number of rods of stone wall that he has built—& the number of tons of hay he now cuts or of bushels of corn or potatoes he raises there—& I feel as if I had got my foot down on to the—solid & sunny earth—the basis of all philosophy—& poetry—& religion even— I have faith that the man who redeemed some acres of land the past summer redeemed also some parts of his character— I shall not expect to find him ever in the almshouse or the prison— He is in fact so far on his way to heaven.— When he took the farm there was not a grafted tree on it—& now he realizes some thing handsome from the sale of the fruit— These—in the absence of other facts are evidence of a certain moral worth.

2 March 1852 ❦ IT WILL SOON BE FORGOTTEN, in these days of stoves, that we used to roast potatoes in the ashes—after the Indian fashion of cooking.

3 March 1841 ❦ IN HEAVEN I HOPE to bake my own bread and clean my own linen.

4 March 1852 ❧ THIS WORLD is a place of business—what an infinite bustle. I am awaked almost every night by the panting of the steam-engine. It interrupts my dreams. There is no Sabbath— It would be glorious to see mankind at leisure for once.

5 March 1853 ❧ THE SECRETARY of the Association for the Ad. of Science—requested me, as he probably has thousands of others—by a printed circular letter from Washington the other day—to fill the blanks against certain questions—among which the most important one was—what branch of science I was specially interested in— Using the term science in the most comprehensive sense possible— Now though I could state to a select few that department of human inquiry which engages me—& should be rejoiced at an opportunity so to do—I felt that it would be to make myself the laughing stock of the scientific community—to describe or attempt to describe to them that branch of science which specially interests me—in as much as they do not believe in a science which deals with the higher law. So I was obliged to speak to their condition and describe to them that poor part of me which alone they can understand. The fact is I am a mystic—a transcendentalist—& a natural philosopher to boot. Now I think—of it—I should have told them at once that I was a transcendentalist—that would have been the shortest way of telling them that they would not understand my explanations.

6 March 1841 ❧ AN HONEST misunderstanding is often the ground of future intercourse.

7 March 1859 ❦ THERE ARE FEW, if any, so coarse and insensible that they are not interested to hear that the bluebird has come. The Irish laborer has learned to distinguish him and report his arrival. It is a part of the news of the season to the lawyer in his office and the mechanic in his shop, as well as to the farmer. One will remember, perchance, to tell you that he saw one a week ago in the next town or county.

8 March 1859 ❦ TO US SNOW AND COLD seem a mere delaying of the spring. How far we are from understanding the value of these things in the economy of Nature!

9 March 1852 ❦ THE SOUND OF WATER falling on rocks and of air falling on trees are very much alike.

10 March 1855 ❦ YOU ARE ALWAYS SURPRISED by the sight of the first spring bird or insect; they seem premature, and there is no such evidence of spring as themselves, so that they literally *fetch* the year about. It is thus when I hear the first robin or bluebird or, looking along the brooks, see the first water-bugs out circling. But you think, They have come, and Nature cannot recede.

11 March 1856 ❦ I WISH SO TO LIVE ever as to derive my satisfactions and inspirations from the commonest events, every-day phenomena, so that what my senses hourly perceive, my daily walk, the conversation of my neighbors, may inspire me, and I may dream of no heaven but that which lies about me. A man may acquire a taste for wine or brandy, and so lose his love for water, but should we not pity him?

Daily Observations

12 March 1853 ❧ DWELL AS NEAR as possible to the channel in which your life flows.

13 March 1853 ❧ As IS THE SUN to the vegetable so is virtue to the bodily health.

14 March 1838 ❧ AFTER ALL the field of battle possesses many advantages over the drawing room. There at least is no room for pretension or excessive ceremony, no shaking of hands or rubbing of noses, which make one doubt your sincerity, but hearty as well as hard handplay— It at least exhibits one of the faces of humanity, the former only a mask.

15 March 1852 ❧ THE AIR is a velvet cushion against which I press my ear— I go forth to make new demands on life. I wish to begin this summer well—to do something in it worthy of it & of me— To transcend my daily routine—& that of my townsmen to have my immortality now—that it be in the *quality* of my daily life. To pay the greatest price—the—greatest tax of any man in Concord—& enjoy the most!! I will give all I am for *my* nobility. I will pay all my days for *my* success. I pray that the life of this spring & summer may ever lie fair in my memory. May I dare as I have never done.— may I persevere as I have never done. May I purify myself anew as with fire & water—soul & body— May my melody not be wanting to the season. May I gird myself to be a hunter of the beautiful that naught escape me— May I attain to a youth never attained I am eager to report the glory of the universe.— may I be worthy to do it— To have got through with regarding human values so as not to be distracted from regarding divine values. It is reasonable that a man should be something worthier at the end of the year than he was at the beginning.

16 March 1842 ❦ THE MOST ATTRACTIVE sentences are not perhaps the wisest, but the surest and soundest. He who uttered them had a right to speak. He did not stand on a rolling stone—but was well assured of his footing—and naturally breathed them without effort. They were spoken in the nick of time.

17 March 1842 ❦ I HAVE BEEN MAKING pencils all day—and then at evening walked to see an old-schoolmate who is going to help make the Welland Canal navigable for ships round Niagara.—

He cannot see any such motives and modes of living as I—Professes not to look beyond the securing of certain "Creature comforts." And so we go silently different ways—with all serenity—I in the still moon light through the village this fair evening to write these thoughts in my journal—and he forsooth to mature his schemes to ends as good maybe but different.

So are we two made while the same stars shine quietly over us. If I or he be wrong—nature yet consents placidly—

18 March 1858 ❦ EACH NEW YEAR is a surprise to us. We find that we had virtually forgotten the note of each bird, and when we hear it again it is remembered like a dream, reminding us of a previous state of existence. How happens it that the associations it awakens are always pleasing, never saddening; reminiscences of our sanest hours? The voice of nature is always encouraging.

19 March 1859 ❦ WE ARE INTERESTED in the phenomena of Nature mainly as children are, or as we are in games of chance. They are more or less exciting. Our appetite for novelty is insatiable. We do not attend to ordinary things, though they are most important, but to extraordinary ones. While it is only moderately hot or cold, or wet or dry, nobody attends to it, but when Nature goes to an extreme in any of these directions we are all on the alert with excitement.

20 March 1855 ❦ TRYING THE OTHER DAY to imitate the honking of geese, I found myself flapping my sides with my elbows, as with wings, and uttering something like the syllables *mow-ack* with a nasal twang and twist in my head; and I produced their note so perfectly in the opinion of the hearers that I thought I might possibly draw a flock down.

21 March 1853 ❦ IT IS A GENIAL & reassuring day—the mere warmth of the west wind amounts almost to balminess. The softness of the air mollifies our own dry & congealed substance. I sit down by a wall to see if I can *muse* again—we become as it were pliant & ductile again to strange but memorable influences—we are led a little way by our genius. We are affected like the earth & yield to the elemental tenderness—winter breaks up within us, the frost is coming out of me & I am heaved like the road   accumulated masses of ice & snow dissolve and thoughts like a freshet pour down unwonted channels.

22 March 1861 ❦ A SEED, which is a plant or tree in embryo, which has the principle of growth, of life, in it, is more important in my eyes, and in the economy of Nature, than the diamond of Kohinoor.

23 March 1856 ❦ I SPEND a considerable portion of my time observing the habits of the wild animals, my brute neighbors. By their various movements and migrations they fetch the year about to me. Very significant are the flight of geese and the migration of suckers, etc. etc. But when I consider that the nobler animals have been exterminated here,—the cougar, panther, lynx, wolverine, wolf, bear, moose, deer, the beaver, the turkey, etc. etc.—I cannot but feel as if I lived in a tamed and, as it were, emasculated country. Would not the motions of those larger and wilder animals have been more significant still? Is it not a maimed and imperfect nature that I am conversant with? As if I were to study a tribe of Indians that had lost all its warriors.

24 March 1842 ❦ THOSE AUTHORS are successful who do not *write down* to others, but make their own taste and judgment their audience. By some strange infatuation we forget that we do not approve what yet we recommend to others.—

It is enough if I please myself with writing— I am then sure of an audience.

25 March 1842 ❦ A MANS LIFE should be as fresh as a river—it should be the same channel but a new water every instant.

26 March 1842 ❦ I WISH TO COMMUNICATE those parts of my life which I would gladly live again myself.

27 March 1853 ❦ TRIED TO SEE the faint-croaking frogs at J. P. Browns pond in the woods— They are remarkably timid & shy—had their noses & eyes out—croaking—but all ceased dove & concealed themselves before I got within a rod of the shore. Stood perfectly still amid the bushes on the shore—before one showed himself—finally 5 or 6 & all eyed me—gradually approached me within 3 feet to reconnoitre and though I waited about ½ hour would not utter a sound nor take their eyes off me— Were plainly affected by curiosity.

28 March 1853 ❦ MY AUNT MARIA asked me to read the life of Dr. Chalmers—which however I did not promise to do. Yesterday, Sunday, she was heard through the partition shouting to my Aunt Jane who is deaf— "Think of it, he stood haf an hour today to hear the frogs croak, and he would'nt read the life of Chalmers—"

29 March 1853 ❦ WOULD IT NOT be well to carry a spy glass in order to watch these shy birds—such as ducks & hawks—? In some respects methinks it would be better than a gun. The latter brings them nearer dead, but the former, alive. You can identify the species better by killing the bird—because it was a dead specimen that was so minutely described—but you can study the habits & appearance best in the living specimen.

30 March 1852 ❦ HAVING OCCASION today to put up a long ladder against the house—I found from the trembling of my nerves—with the exertion that I had not exercised that part of my system this winter. How much I may have lost. It would do me good to go forth & work hard & sweat. Though the frost is nearly out of the ground the winter has not broken up in me. It is a backward season with me. Perhaps we grow older & older till we no longer sympathize with the revolution of the seasons—& our winters never break up.

31 March 1842 ❧ THE REALLY EFFICIENT laborer will be found not to crowd his day with work but will saunter to his task surrounded by a wide halo of ease and leisure— There will be a wide margin for relaxation to his day— He is only earnest to secure the kernels of time—and does not exaggerate the value of the husk.

Why should the hen set all day—she can lay but one egg— and besides she will not have picked up materials for a new one.— Those who work much do not work hard.

APRIL

1 April 1852 ❦ SAT AWHILE before sun-set on the rocks in Saw Mill Brook— A brook need not be large to afford us pleasure by its sands & meanderings and falls & their various accompaniments. It is not so much size that we want as picturesque beauty & harmony. If the sound of its fall fills my ear it is enough.

2 April 1853 ❦ WE CANNOT well afford not to see the geese go over a single spring, and so commence our year regularly.

3 April 1853 ❦ THE LAST TWO TRIBUNES I have not looked at— I have no time to read newspapers— If you chance to live & move and have your being in that thin stratum—in which the events which make the news transpire—thinner than the paper on which it is printed—then those things will fill the world for you—but if you soar above or dive below that plain—you cannot remember nor be reminded of them.

4 April 1853 ❦ THE OTHER DAY when I had been standing perfectly still some 10 minutes looking at a willow which had just blossomed some rods in the rear of Martial Miles' house— I felt eyes on my back & turning round suddenly saw the heads of two men who had stolen out of the house and were watching me over a rising ground as fixedly as I the willow. They were studying Man, which is said to be the proper study of mankind—I nature—& yet when detected they felt the cheapest of the two.

5 April 1853 ❦ The blue-bird comes to us bright in his vernal dress as a bridegroom.

6 April 1856 ❦ Just beyond Wood's Bridge, I hear the pewee. With what confidence after the lapse of many months, I come out to this waterside, some warm and pleasant spring morning, and, listening, hear, from farther or nearer, through the still concave of the air, the note of the first pewee! If there is one within half a mile, it will be here, and I shall be sure to hear its simple notes from those trees, borne over the water.

7 April 1853 ❦ If you make the least correct observation of nature this year—you will have occasion to repeat it with illustrations the next, and the season & life itself is prolonged.

8 April 1859 ❦ What a pitiful business is the fur trade, which has been pursued now for so many ages, for so many years by famous companies which enjoy a profitable monopoly and control a large portion of the earth's surface, unweariedly pursuing and ferreting out small animals by the aid of all the loafing class tempted by rum and money, that you may rob some little fellow-creature of its coat to adorn or thicken your own, that you may get a fashionable covering in which to hide your head, or a suitable robe in which to dispense justice to your fellow-men! Regarded from the philosopher's point of view, it is precisely on a level with rag and bone picking in the streets of the cities.

9 April 1853 ❦ The whole meadow resounds—probably from one end of the river to the other this evening with this faint stertorous breathing. It is the waking up of the meads. Louder than all is heard the shrill peep of the hylodes—& the hovering note of the snipe circling invisible above them all.

10 April 1854 ❦ I BOUGHT ME a spy-glass some weeks since. I buy but few things—and those not till long after I began to want them—so that when I do get them I am prepared to make a perfect use of them and extract their whole sweet.

11 April 1857 ❦ IF SALMON, shad and alewives were pressing up our river now, as formerly they were, a good part of the villagers would thus, no doubt, be drawn to the brink at this season. Many inhabitants of the neighborhood of the ponds in Lakeville, Freetown, Fairhaven, etc., have petitioned the legislature for permission to connect Little Quitticus Pond with the Acushnet River by digging, so that the herring can come up into it. The very fishes in countless schools are driven out of a river by the *improvements* of the civilized man, as the pigeon and other fowls out of the air. I can hardly imagine a greater change than this produced by the influence of man in nature. Our Concord River is a dead stream in more senses than we had supposed. In what sense now does the spring ever come to the river, when the sun is not reflected from the scales of a single salmon, shad or alewife?

12 April 1858 ❦ RETURNING on the railroad, the noon train down passed us opposite the old maid Hosmer's house. In the woods just this side, we came upon a partridge standing on the track, between the rails over which the cars had just passed. She had evidently been run down, but, though a few small feathers were scattered along for a dozen rods beyond her, and she looked a little ruffled, she was apparently more disturbed in mind than in body. I took her up and carried her one side to a safer place. At first she made no resistance, but at length fluttered out of my hands and ran two or three feet. I had to take her up again and carry and drive her further off, and left her standing with head erect as at first, as if beside herself. She was not lame, and I suspect no wing was broken. I did not suspect that this swift wild bird was ever run down by the cars. We have an account in the newspapers of every cow and calf that is run over, but not of the various wild creatures who meet with that accident. It may be many generations before the partridges learn to give the cars a sufficiently wide berth.

13 April 1852 ❦ A DRIVING SNOW STORM in the night & still raging—5 or 6 inches deep on a level at 7Am. All birds are turned into snow birds. Trees and houses have put on the aspect of winter The travellers carriage wheels, the farmer's wagon are converted into white disks of snow through which the spokes hardly appear. But it is good now to stay in the house & read & write. We do not now go wandering all abroad & dissipated—but the imprisoning storm condenses our thoughts— I can hear the clock tick as not in pleasant weather— My life is enriched— I love to hear the wind howl. I have a fancy for sitting with my book or paper—in some mean & apparently unfavorable place—in the kitchen for instance where the work is going on—rather a little cold than comfortable— — My thoughts are of more worth in such places than they would be in a well-furnished & warmed studio.

14 April 1852 ❦ I HAVE BEEN OUT every afternoon this past winter, as usual, in sun & wind snow & rain, without being particularly tanned— This *forenoon* I walked in the woods and felt the heat reflected from the snow so sensibly in some parts of the cut on the R R that I was reminded of those oppressive days 2 or 3 summers ago when the laborers were obliged to work by night— Well since I have come home—, this afternoon & evening,—I find that I am suddenly tanned even to making the skin of my nose sore.

15 April 1858 ❦ THE NATURALIST accomplishes a great deal by patience, more perhaps than by activity. He must take his position, and then wait and watch.

16 April 1854 ❦ WHEN I MEET one of my neighbors these days who is ridiculously stately being offended—I say in my mind Farewell—. I will wait till you get your manners off— Why make politeness of so much consequence when you are ready to assassinate with a word. I do not like any better to be assassinated with a rapier, than to be knocked down with a bludgeon. You are so grand that I cannot get within ten feet of you. Why will men so try to impose on one another? Why not be simple & pass for what they are worth only? O such thin skins, such crockery, as I have to deal with!

17 April 1855 ❦ NO MATTER what pains you take, probably— undoubtedly—an insect will have found the first flower before you.

18 April 1852 ❦ FOR THE FIRST TIME I perceive this spring that the year is a circle— I see distinctly the spring arc thus far. It is drawn with a firm line. Every incident is a parable of the great teacher.

19 April 1852 ❦ To SEE WILD LIFE—you must go forth at a wild season. When it rains & blows keeping men in-doors then the lover of nature must forth.

20 April 1854 ❦ I FIND SOME ADVANTAGE in describing the experience of a day on the day following. At this distance it is more ideal like the landscape seen with the head inverted or reflections in water.

21 April 1852 ❦ ON THE E SIDE of Ponkawtassett I hear a robin singing cheerily from some perch in the wood—in the midst of the rain.— where the scenery is now wild & dreary— His song a singular antagonism & offset to the storm— As if nature said "have faith, these *two* things I can do." It sings with power—like a bird of great faith—that sees the bright future through the dark present—to reassure the race of man—like one to whom many talents were given & who will improve its talents. They are sounds to make a dying man live. They sing not their despair. It is a pure immortal melody.

22 April 1851 ❦ IT IS NOT THE INVITATION which I hear, but which I feel, that I obey.

23 April 1857 ❦ How RARELY a man's love for nature becomes a ruling principle with him, like a youth's affection for a maiden, but more enduring! All nature is my bride. That nature which to one is a stark and ghastly solitude is a sweet, tender, and genial society to another.

24 April 1859 ❧ WE MUST NOT BE GOVERNED by rigid rules, as by the almanac, but let the season rule us. The moods and thoughts of man are revolving just as steadily and incessantly as nature's. Nothing must be postponed. Take time by the forelock. Now or never! You must live in the present, launch yourself on every wave, find your eternity in each moment. Fools stand on their island opportunities and look toward another land.

25 April 1841 ❧ WHEN I HEAR a robin sing at sunset—I cannot help contrasting the equanimity of nature with the bustle and impatience of man We return from the lyceum and caucus with such stir and excitement—as if a crisis were at hand but no natural scene or sound sympathizes with us, for nature is always silent and unpretending as at the break of day. She but rubs her eye lids.

26 April 1841 ❧ THE CHARM of the Indian to me is that he stands free and unconstrained in nature—is her inhabitant— and not her guest—and wears her easily and gracefully. But the civilized man has the habits of the house.

27 April 1854 ❧ THE WOOD-THRUSH afar—so superior a strain to that of other birds. I was doubting if it would affect me as of yore but it did measurably— I did not believe there could be such differences. This is the gospel according to the woodthrush. He makes a sabbath out of a week day— I could go to hear him—could buy a pew in his church—

28 April 1856 ❧ HOW DARING, even rash, Nature appears, who sends out butterflies so early!

29 April 1851 ❧ It often happens that a man is more humanely related to a cat or dog than to any human being. What bond is it relates us to any animal we keep in the house but the bond of affection? In a degree we grow to love one another.

30 April 1852 ❧ The season advances by fits & starts   you would not believe that there could be so many degrees to it— If you have had foul & cold weather still some advance has been made as you find when the fair weather comes—new lieferungs of warmth & summeriness—which make yesterday seem far off—& the dog days of mid-summer incredibly nearer.

MAY

1 May 1859 ❧ THE CATECHISM says that the chief end of man is to glorify God and enjoy him forever, which of course is applicable mainly to God as seen in his works. Yet the only account of its beautiful insects—butterflies, etc.—which God has made and set before us which the State ever thinks of spending any money on is the account of those which are injurious to vegetation! This is the way we glorify God and enjoy him forever. Come out here and behold a thousand painted butterflies and other beautiful insects which people the air, then go to the libraries and see what kind of prayer and glorification of God is there recorded. Massachusetts has published her report on "Insects Injurious to Vegetation," and our neighbor the "Noxious Insects of New York." We have attended to the evil and said nothing about the good. This is looking a gift horse in the mouth with a vengeance. Children are attracted by the beauty of butterflies, but their parents and legislators deem it an idle pursuit. The parents remind me of the devil, but the children of God. Though God may have pronounced his work good, we ask, "Is it poisonous?"

2 May 1859 ❧ I FEEL NO DESIRE to go to California or Pike's Peak, but I often think at night with inexpressible satisfaction and yearning of the *arrowheadiferous* sands of Concord. I have often spent whole afternoons, especially in the spring, pacing back and forth over a sandy field, looking for these relics of a race. This is the gold which our sands yield.

3 May 1852 ❧ The little peepers have much the greatest apparatus for peeping of any frogs that I know. Frogs are the birds of the night.

4 May 1857 ❧ Perhaps the most generally interesting event at present is a perfectly warm and pleasant day. It affects the greatest number, the well out of doors and the sick in chambers. No wonder the weather is the universal theme of conversation.

5 May 1846 ❧ The subject of sex is a most remarkable one— since though it occupies the thoughts of all so much, and our lives & characters are so affected by the consequences which spring from this source— Yet mankind as it were tacitly agrees to be silent about it—at least the sexes do one to another.

6 May 1851 ❧ How important is a constant intercourse with nature and the contemplation of natural phenomenon to the preservation of Moral & intellectual health. The discipline of the schools or of business—can never impart such serenity to the mind.

7 May 1855 ❧ Scared up two gray squirrels in the Holden wood, which ran glibly up the tallest trees on the opposite side to me, and leaped across from the extremity of the branches to the next trees, and so on very fast ahead of me. Remembering— aye, aching with—my experience in climbing trees this afternoon and morning, I could not but admire their exploits. To see them travelling with so much swiftness and ease that road over which I climbed a few feet with such painful exertion!

8 May 1852 ❦ No TARTS that I ever tasted at any table—possessed such a refreshing—cheering—encouraging acid—that literally put the heart in you & set you on edge for this worlds experiences—bracing the spirit—as the cranberries I have plucked in the meadows in the Spring. They cut the winters phlegm & now I can swallow another year of this world without other sauce.

9 May 1852 ❦ Is NOT ALL the summer akin to a paradise

10 May 1854 ❦ IN BOSTON yesterday an ornithologist said significantly—"if you held the bird in your hand"—but I would rather hold it in my affections—

11 May 1853 ❦ How MANY little birds—of the warbler family are busy now about the opening buds while I sit by the spring— They are almost as much a part of the tree as its blossoms & leaves. They come and give it voice.

12 May 1850 ❦ I TOO REVIVE as does the grass after rain—

13 May 1856 ❦ . . . IF YOU LOOK through a thick pine wood, even the exclusively pitch pine ones, you will detect many little oaks, birches, etc., sprung probably from seeds carried into the thicket by squirrels, etc., and blown thither, but which are overshadowed and choked by the pines. This planting under the shelter of the pines may be carried on annually, and the plants annually die, but when the pines are cleared off, the oaks, etc., having got just the start they want, and now secured favorable conditions, immediately spring up to trees. Scarcely enough allowance has been made for the agency of squirrels and birds in dispersing seeds.

14 May 1852 ❧ MOST MEN can be easily transplanted from here there, for they have so little root—no tap root—or their roots penetrate so little way—that you can thrust a shovel quite under them and take them up roots and all.

15 May 1853 ❧ THE FIRST CRICKETS chirrup which I have chanced to hear now falls on my ear—& makes me forget all else—all else is a thin & moveable crust down to that depth where he resides eternally. He already fore tels autumn—deep under the dry border of some rock in this hill side he sits—& makes the finest singing of birds outward & insignificant—his own song is so much deeper & more significant. His voice has set me thinking—philosophizing —moralizing at once — it is not so wildly melodious but it is wiser & more mature than that of the wood thrush—with this elixir I see clear through the summer now to autumn & and any summer work seems frivolous—

16 May 1852 ❧ EVEN OUR RIVER SHELLS will have some lilack purple or green tints telling of distant skies—like shells from the Indies. How did these beautiful rain bow tints get into the shell of the fresh-water clam buried in the mud at the bottom of our dark river? Even the sea-bottom tells of the upper skies.

17 May 1858 ❧ THIS RAIN IS GOOD for thought. It is especially agreeable to me as I enter the wood and hear the soothing dripping on the leaves. It domiciliates me in nature. The woods are the more like a house for the rain; the few slight noises sound more hollow in them; the birds hop nearer; the very trees seem still and pensive. The clouds are but a higher roof.

18 May 1851 ❦ It seems to take but one summer day to fetch the summer in.

19 May 1856 ❦ As I sail up the reach of the Assabet above Dock Rock with a fair wind, a traveller riding along the highway is watching my sail while he hums a tune. How inspiring and elysian it is to hear when the traveller or the laborer from a call to his horse or the murmur of ordinary conversation rises into song! It paints the landscape suddenly as no agriculture, no flowery crop that can be raised. It is at once another land, the abode of poetry. I am always thus affected when I hear in the fields any singing or instrumental music at the end of the day. It implies a different life and pursuits than the ordinary. As he looked at my sail, I listened to his singing. Perchance they were equally poetic, and we repaid each other.

20 May 1856 ❦ I hear it in mid-afternoon, muttering, crashing in the muggy air in mid-heaven, a little south of the village as I go through it, like the tumbling down of piles of boards, and get a few sprinkles in the sun. Nature has found her hoarse summer voice again, like the lowing of a cow let out to pasture. It is Nature's rutting season. Even as the birds sing tumultuously and glance by with fresh and brilliant plumage, so now is Nature's grandest voice heard, and her sharpest flashes seen. The air has resumed its voice, and the lightning, like a yellow spring flower, illumines the dark banks of the clouds. All the pregnant earth is bursting into life like a mildew, accompanied with noise and fire and tumult.

21 May 1854 ❧ Cob-webs on grass the first I have noticed—
this is one of the *late* phenomena of Spring— These little dewy
nets or gauze—a faery's washing—spread out in the night are
associated with the finest days of the year— Days long enough
& fair enough for the worthiest deeds. When these begin to be
seen then is not summer come?

22 May 1853 ❧ When yesterday Sophia & I were rowing
past Mr Pritchards Land where the river is bordered by a row
of elms & low willows at 6 Pm—we heard a singular note of distress as it were from a cat bird. a loud, vibrating, cat bird sort of
note—as if the cat birds mew were imitated by a smart vibrating spring. Blackbirds & others were flitting about apparently
attracted by it— At first thinking it was merely some peevish
catbird or red-wing—I was disregarding it but on 2nd thought
turned the bows to the shore—looking into the trees as well
as over the shore—thinking some bird might be in distress—
caught by a snake or in a forked twig. The hovering birds dis-
persed at my approached—the note of distress sounded louder &
nearer as I approached the shore covered with low osiers— The
sound came from the ground not from the trees— I saw a little
black animal making haste to meet the boat under the osiers—a
young muskrat —?—a mink?—no it was a little dot of a kitten
It was scarcely 6 inches long from the face to the base—or I
might as well say the tip of the tail—for the latter was a short
sharp pyramid perfectly perpendicular—but not swelled in the
least— It was a very handsome and very precocious kitten—in
perfectly good condition—its breadth being considerably more
than 1/3 of its length. Ceasing its mewing it came scrambling
over the stones as fast as its weak legs would permit straight

to me. I took it up & dropped it into the boat—but while I was pushing off it ran the length of the boat to Sophia—who held it while we rowed homeward.

23 May 1853 ❦ THE POET MUST BRING to nature the smooth mirror in which she is to be reflected. He must be something superior to her something more than natural. He must furnish equanimity.

24 May 1860 ❦ How PERFECTLY NEW and fresh the world is seen to be, when we behold a myriad sparkles of brilliant white sunlight on a rippled stream! So remote from dust and decay, more bright than the flash of an eye.

25 May 1851 ❦ MEN WILL PAY something to look into a travelling showman's box—but not to look upon the fairest prospects on the earth.

26 May 1853 ❦ NOW IS THE TIME to walk in low damp maple copses & see the tender luxuriant foliage that has pushed up mushroom like—before the sun has come to harden it—the ferns of various species & in various stages—some now in their most perfect & beautiful condition completely unfolded tender & delicate but perfect in all their details—far more than any lace work—the most elaborate leaf we have. So flat just from the laundry as if pressed by some invisible flatiron in the air.

27 May 1841 ❧ I SIT IN MY BOAT on walden—playing the flute this evening—and see the perch, which I seem to have charmed, hovering around me—and the moon travelling over the ribbed bottom—and feel that nothing but the wildest imagination can conceive of the manner of life we are living. Nature is a wizzard. The Concord nights are stranger than the Arabian nights.

28 May 1854 ❧ IT WOULD BE WORTH the while to ask ourselves weekly—Is our life innocent enough? Do we live *inhumanely*— toward man or beast—in thought or act? To be serene & successful we must be at one with the universe. The least conscious & needless injury inflicted on any creature—is to its extent a suicide. What peace—or life—can a murderer have?

29 May 1854 ❧ I SEE THE THE COURT HOUSE full of armed men holding prisoner & trying a *Man* to find out if he is not really a *Slave*. It is a question about which there is great doubt.

It is really the trial of Massachusetts—every moment that she hesitates to set this man free—she is convicted. The Commissioner on her case is God.

30 May 1857 ❧ THE BLUE SKY is never more celestial to our eyes than when it is first seen here and there between the clouds at the end of a storm,—a sign of speedy fair weather.

31 May 1850 ❧ THERE IS A SWEET wild world which lies along the strain of the wood thrush—the rich intervales which border the stream of its song—more thoroughly genial to my nature than any other.

JUNE

1 June 1854 ❧ Now I see gentle men and ladies sitting at anchor in boats on the lakes in the calm afternoons—under parasols—making use of nature—Not always accumulating money. The farmer hoeing is wont to look with scorn & pride on a man sitting in a motionless boat a whole half day—but he does not realize that the object of his own labor is perhaps merely to add another dollar to his heap—nor through what coarseness & inhumanity to his family & servants he often accomplishes this.

2 June 1853 ❧ 3 ½ Am When I awake I hear the low universal chirping or twittering of the chip-birds—like the bursting bead on the surface of the uncorked day. Firrst come first served—you must taste the first glass of the days necter—if you would get all the spirit of it.

3 June 1857 ❧ I have several friends and acquaintances who are very good companions in the house or for an afternoon walk, but whom I cannot make up my mind to make a longer excursion with; for I discover, all at once, that they are too gentlemanly in manners, dress, and all their habits. I see in my mind's eye that they wear black coats, considerable starched linen, glossy hats and shoes, and it is out of the question. It is a great disadvantage for a traveller to be a gentleman of this kind; he is so ill-treated, only a prey to landlords. It would be too much of a circumstance to enter a strange town or house with such a companion. You could not travel incognito; you might get into the papers. You should travel as a common man.

4 June 1852 ❦ THE BIRDS SING at dawn. What sounds to be awakened by! If only our sleep—our dreams are such as to harmonize with the song—the warbling of the birds ushering in the day.

5 June 1857 ❦ I AM INTERESTED in each contemporary plant in my vicinity, and have attained to a certain acquaintance with the larger ones. They are cohabitants with me of this part of the planet, and they bear familiar names. Yet how essentially wild they are! as wild, really, as those strange fossil plants whose impressions I see on my coal. Yet I can imagine that some race gathered those too with as much admiration, and knew them as intimately as I know these, that even they served for a language of the sentiments.

6 June 1857 ❦ EACH SEASON is but an infinitesimal point. It no sooner comes than it is gone. It has no duration. It simply gives a tone and hue to my thought. Each annual phenomenon is a reminiscence and a prompting. Our thoughts and sentiments answer to the revolutions of the seasons, as two cog-wheels fit into each other. We are conversant with only one point of contact at a time, from which we receive a prompting and impulse and instantly pass to a new season or point of contact. A year is made up of a certain series and number of sensations and thoughts which have their language in nature.

7 June 1851 ❦ ONE OF THOSE GENTLE straight down rainy days—when the rain begins by spotting the cultivated fields as if shaken from a pepper-box—a fishing day—when I see one neighbor after another—having donned his oil cloth suit walking or riding past with a fish-pole—having struck work—a day & an employment to make philosophers of them all.

8 June 1850 ❧ THE CARS come & go with such regularity & precision—and the whistle & rumble are heard so far—that town clocks & family clocks are already half dispensed with—And it is easy to foresee that one extensive well conducted & orderly institution like a rail-road will keep time & order for a whole country. The startings & arrivals of the cars are the epochs in a village day.

9 June 1854 ❧ I SHOULD LIKE TO KNOW the birds of the woods better. What birds inhabit our woods. I hear their various notes ringing through them. What musicians compose our woodland quire. They must be forever strange & interesting to me.

10 June 1853 ❧ Now METHINKS the birds begin to sing less tumultuously—with as the weather grows more constantly warm morning—& noon & evening songs—& suitable recesses in the concert.

11 June 1855 ❧ WHEN I WOULD GO a-visiting I find that I go off the fashionable street—not being inclined to change my dress—to where man meets man and not polished shoe meets shoe.

12 June 1851 ❧ LISTEN TO MUSIC religiously as if it were the last strain you might hear.

13 June 1854 ❧ IF IT RAINS HARD I will run my boat ashore turn it over & get under it— I will not turn back—my afternoon shall not be interrupted by a thunder shower.

14 June 1851 ❧ How MODERATE—deliberate is nature—how gradually the shades of night gather & deepen giving man ample leisure to bid farewell to day—conclude his day's affairs & prepare for slumber.— The twilight seems out of proportion to the length of the day—

15 June 1852 ❧ How RAPIDLY new flowers infold—as if nature would get through her work too soon. One has as much as he can do to observe how flowers successively unfold. It is a flowery revolution to which but few attend. Hardly too much attention can be bestowed on flowers.

16 June 1854 ❧ WHAT CONFIRMATION of our hopes is in the fragrance of the water lily. I shall not so soon despair of the world for it notwithstanding slavery—& the cowardice & want of principle of the North— It suggests that the time may come when man's deeds will smell as sweet—

17 June 1853 ❧ IF A MAN WALKS in the woods—for love of them & see his fellows with impartial eye afar—for half his days—he is esteemed a loafer—but if he spends his whole day as a speculator shearing off those woods he is esteemed industrious & enterprising—making earth bald before its time.

18 June 1854 ❧ As FOR ASKING the south to grant us the trial by jury in the case of run away slaves—It is as if—seeing a righteous man sent to Hell we should run together & petition the Devil first to grant him a trial by jury—forgetting that there is another power to be petitioned—there there is another law and other precedents.

19 June 1852 ❦ O MAY MY WORDS be verdurous & sempiternal as the hills.

20 June 1846 ❦ A RIVER or any water especially if placid is a place of singular enchantment— Nature exhibits a fabulous wealth there for not only are you struck by the weedy luxuriance of the bottom—but this is doubled by the flection of all the fertility upon the banks.

21 June 1857 ❦ WHEN MR. POOL, the Doorkeeper of the House of Representatives,—if that is his name and title,—who makes out a list of the Representatives and their professions, asked him his business, he answered, 'Fisherman.' At which Pool was disturbed and said that no representative had ever called himself a fisherman before. It would not do to print it so. And so Atwood is put down as 'Master Mariner'!! So much for American democracy. I reminded him that Fisherman had been a title of honor with a large party ever since the Christian Era at least. When next we have occasion to speak of the apostles I suppose we should call them 'Master Mariners'!

22 June 1851 ❦ ARE OUR SERENE MOMENTS mere foretastes of heaven joys gratuitously vouchsafed to us as a consolation—or simply a transient realization of what might be the whole tenor of our lives?

23 June 1840 ❦ HE IS THE TRUE ARTIST whose life is his material—every stroke of the chisel must enter his own flesh and bone, and not grate dully on marble.

24 June 1852 ❧ A SKY WITHOUT CLOUDS is a meadow without flowers— A sea without sails.

25 June 1840 ❧ LET ME SEE NO OTHER CONFLICT but with prosperity—

26 June 1856 ❧ HEARD OF, and sought out, the hut of Martha Simons, the only pure-blooded Indian left about New Bedford. . . . The question she answered with most interest was, 'What do you call that plant?' and I reached her the aletris from my hat. She took it, looked at it a moment, and said, 'That's husk-root. It's good to put into bitters for a weak stomach.' The last year's light-colored and withered leaves surround the present green star like a husk. This must be the origin of the name. Its root is described as intensely bitter. I ought to have had my hat full of plants.

A conceited old Quaker minister, her neighbor, told me with a sanctified air, 'I think that the Indians were human beings; dost thee not think so?' He only convinced me of his doubt and narrowness.

27 June 1852 ❧ A HEALTHY & REFINED NATURE would always derive pleasure from the landscape. As long as the bodily vigor lasts man sympathizes with nature—

28 June 1852 ❧ THERE ARE METEOROLOGISTS—but who keeps a record of the fairer sunsets? While men are recording the direction of the wind they neglect to record the beauty of the sun set or the rain bow.

29 June 1851 ❧ THE VOICE OF THE CRICKETS heard at noon from deep in the grass allies day to night— It is unaffected by sun & moon. It is a mid-night sound heard at noon—a midday sound heard at mid night.

30 June 1852 ❧ A LOVER OF NATURE is preeminently a lover of man. If I have no friend—what is nature to me? She ceases to be morally significant.

JULY

1 July 1852 ❧ I DRANK some high colored water from a little stream in the meadow—for I love to drink the water of the meadow or the river I pass the day on—& so get eyes to see it with—

2 July 1858 ❧ THERE IS SOMETHING in the scenery of a broad river equivalent to culture and civilization. Its channel conducts our thoughts as well as bodies to classic and famous ports, and allies us to all that is fair and great.

3 July 1840 ❧ DO NOT THOUGHTS and men's lives enrich the earth and change the aspect of things as much as a new growth of wood?

4 July 1858 ❧ IT IS FAR MORE INDEPENDENT to travel on foot.

5 July 1852 ❧ I KNOW A MAN who never speaks of the sexual relation but jestingly, though it is a subject to be approached only with reverence & affection. What can be the character of that man's love?

6 July 1852 ❧ FOR BIRDS' NESTS & berries give me a child's eyes.

7 July 1851 ❧ WITH A CERTAIN WARINESS, but not without a slight shudder at the danger oftentimes, I perceive how near I had come to admitting into my mind the details of some trivial affair, as a case at court— And I am astonished to observe how willing men are to lumber their minds with such rubbish—to permit idle rumors tales incidents even of an insignificant kind—to intrude upon what should be the sacred ground of the thoughts

8 July 1852 ❧ I AM INCLINED to think bathing almost one of the necessaries of life but it is surprising how indifferent some are to it. What a coarse foul lusty life we lead compared even with the South Sea Islanders in some respects. Truant boys steal away to bathe—but the farmers who most need it rarely dip their bodies into the streams . . .

9 July 1851 ❧ WHAT CAN BE more impressive than to look up a noble river just at evening—one perchance which you have never explored—& behold its placid waters reflecting the woods—& sky lapsing inaudibly toward the ocean—to behold as a lake—but know it as a river—tempting the beholder to explore it—& his own destiny at once.

10 July 1852 ❧ I WONDER if any Roman emperor ever indulged in such luxury as this—of walking up & down a river in torrid weather with only a hat to shade the head.

11 July 1851 ❧ I HEAR THE SOUND of Heywood's brook falling into Fair Haven Pond—inexpressibly refreshing to my senses—it seems to flow through my very bones.— I hear it with insatiable thirst— It allays some sandy heat in me— It affects my circulations—methinks my arteries have sympathy with it What is it I hear but the pure water falls within me in the circulation of my blood—the streams that fall into my heart?— what mists do I ever see but such as hang over—& rise from my blood— The sound of this gurgling water—running thus by night as by day—falls on all my dashes—fills all my buckets—overflows my float boards—turns all the machinery of my nature makes me a flume—a sluice way to the springs of nature—

12 July 1840 ❧ WHEN I SEE a fine lady or gentleman dressed to the top of the fashion, I wonder what they would do if an earthquake should happen; or a fire suddenly break out, for they seem to have counted only on fair weather, and that things will go smoothly and without jostling. Those curls and jewels so nicely adjusted expect an unusual deference from the elements.

13 July 1857 ❧ THE PRICE OF FRIENDSHIP is the total surrender of yourself; no lesser kindness, no ordinary attentions and offerings will buy it.

14 July 1845 ❧ THERE CAN BE NO really *black* melan-choly to him who lives in the midst of nature, and has still his senses.

15 July 1860 ❧ IT SEEMED TO ME yesterday that the foliage had attained its maximum of darkness, and as I ascended the hill at eve the hickories looked even autumnal.

16 July 1851 ❧ MAY I SO LIVE and refine my life as fitting myself for a society ever higher than I actually enjoy. May I treat myself tenderly as I would treat the most innocent child whom I love—may I treat children & my friends as my newly discovered self—

17 July 1860 ❦ The nighthawk's ripping sound, heard overhead these days, reminds us that the sky is, as it were, a roof, and that our world is limited on that side, it being reflected as from a roof back to earth.

18 July 1858 ❦ The convenience of the traveller is very little consulted. He merely has the privilege of crossing somebody's farm by a particular narrow and maybe unpleasant path. The individual retains all other rights,—as to trees and fruits, and wash of the road, etc. On the other hand, these should belong to mankind inalienably. The road should be of ample width and adorned with trees expressly for the use of the traveller. There should be broad recesses in it, especially at springs and watering-places, where he can turn out and rest, or camp if he will. I feel commonly as if I were condemned to drive through somebody's cow-yard or huckleberry pasture by a narrow lane, and if I make a fire by the roadside to boil my hasty pudding, the farmer comes running over to see if I am not burning up his stuff.

19 July 1851 ❦ Let a man step to the music which he hears however measured.

20 July 1851 ❦ I meet one late in the afternoon going to the river with his basket on his arm & his pole in hand—not ambitious to catch pickerel this time, but he thinks he may perhaps get a mess of small fish. These kind of values are real & important—though but little appreciated—& he is not a wise legislator who underrates them and allows the bridge to be built low so as to prevent the passage of small boats. The town is but little conscious how much interest it has in the river—might vote it away anyday thoughtlessly.

21 July 1851 ❧ WITH MOST MEN life is postponed to some trivial business & so therefore is heaven.

22 July 1860 ❧ THE FARMER accustomed to look at his crops from a mercenary point of view is not aware how beautiful they are.

23 July 1852 ❧ EVERYMAN SAYS his dog will not touch you— Look out nevertheless.

24 July 1852 ❧ I SYMPATHIZE with weeds perhaps more than with the crop they choke—they express so much vigor—they are the truer crop which the earth more willingly bears—

25 July 1851 ❧ IT IS FOLLY to attempt to educate children within a city—the first step must be to remove them out of it.

26 July 1840 ❧ WHEN I CONSIDER how, after sunset, the stars come out gradually in troops from behind the hills and woods, I confess that I could not have contrived a more curious and inspiring night.

27 July 1852 ❧ I SHOULD LIKE TO ASK the assessors what is the value of that blue *mt* range in the NW horizon to Concord— and see if they would laugh or seriously set about calculating it. How poor comparatively should we be without it!

28 July 1854 ❧ METHINKS THE SEASON culminated about the middle of this month—That the year was of indefinite promise before— —but that, after the 1st intense heats we postponed the fulfillment of many of our hopes for this year—& having as it were attained the ridge of the summer—commenced to descend the long slope toward winter—the afternoon & down hill of the year— Last evening it was much cooler—& I heard a decided fall sound of crickets—

29 July 1853 ❧ PERCHANCE the moon shines sometimes merely to tempt men forth to view creation by night—but soon wanes to warn them that day is the season appointed for their labors—

30 July 1852 ❧ DO NOT ALL FLOWERS that blossom after mid. July remind us of the fall? After midsummer we have a belated feeling as if we had all been idlers—& are forward to see in each sight—& hear in each sound some presage of the fall.— just as in mid. age man anticipates the end of life.

31 July 1840 ❧ ANY MELODIOUS SOUND apprises me of the infinite wealth of God.

AUGUST

1 August 1860 ❦ HOW MUCH OF BEAUTY—of color, as well as form—on which our eyes daily rest goes unperceived by us! No one but a botanist is like to distinguish nicely the different shades of green with which the open surface of the earth is clothed,—not even a landscape-painter if he does not know the species of sedges and grasses which paint it.

2 August 1854 ❦ I MUST CULTIVATE privacy. It is very dissipating to be with people too much. As C. says, it takes the edge off a man's thoughts to have been much in society— I can not spare my moonlight & my *mts* for the best of man I am likely to get in exchange—
I am inclined now for a pensive evening walk.

3 August 1857 ❦ IT IS SO MUCH the more desirable at this season to breathe the raspberry air of Maine.

4 August 1838 ❦ WHATEVER OF PAST or present wisdom has published itself to the world, is palpable falsehood till it come and utter itself by my side.

5 August 1851 ❦ AS THE TWILIGHT deepens and the moonlight is more & more bright—I begin to distinguish myself who I am & where—as my walls contract I become more collected & composed & sensible of my own existence—as when a lamp is brought into a dark apartment & I see who the company are. With the coolness & the mild silvery light I recover some sanity—my thoughts are more distinct moderated & tempered— Reflection is more possible while the day goes by. The intense light of the sun unfits me for meditation makes me wander in my thought—my life is too diffuse & dissipated— routine succeeds & prevails over us—the trivial has greater power then & most at noon day the most trivial hour of the 24. I am sobered by the moonlight— I bethink myself— It is like a cup of cold water to a thirsty man. The moonlight is more favorable to meditation than sun-light.

6 August 1852 ❦ METHINKS we do ourselves at any rate some what tire of the season—& observe less attentively and with less interest the opening of new flowers—and the song of the birds— It is the signs of the fall that affect us most. It is hard to live in the summer content with it.

7 August 1854 ❦ THERE IS A LIGHT on the earth & leaves as if they were burnished— It is the glistening autumnal side of Summer— I feel a cool vein in the breeze—which braces my thought—& I pass with pleasure over sheltered & sunny por- tions of the sand where the summers heat is undiminished—& I realize what a friend I am losing.

8 August 1859 ❦ THE RIVER, now that it is so clear and sunny, is better than any aquarium. Standing up and pushing gently up the stream, or floating yet more quietly down it, I can, in some places, see the secrets of half the river and its inhabitants,—the common and familiar bream with the dusty light reflected from its fins, the vigorous-looking perch, tiger-like among fishes (I notice that many of the perch are poised head downward, peeping under the rocks), the motionless pickerel with reticulated back and sides, as it were the seed-vessel of a water plant, eyes set far back. It is an enchanter's wand ready to surprise you with life.

9 August 1858 ❦ IT IS SURPRISING what a tissue of trifles and crudities make the daily news. For one event of interest there are nine hundred and ninety-nine insignificant, but about the same stress is laid on the last as on the first. The newspapers have just told me that the transatlantic telegraph-cable is laid. That is important, but they instantly proceed to inform me how the news was received in every larger town in the United States,— how many guns they fired, or how high they jumped,—in New York, and Milwaukee, and Sheboygan; and the boys and girls, old and young, at the corners of the streets are reading it all with glistening eyes, down to the very last scrap, not omitting what they did at New Rochelle and Evansville. And all the speeches are reported, and some think of collecting them into a volume!!!

10 August 1856 ❦ I GO ACROSS lots like a hunting dog. With what tireless energy and abandonment they dash through the brush and up the sides of hills! I meet two white foxhounds, led by an old red one. How full of it they are! How their tails work! They are not tied to paths; they burst forth from the thickest shrub oak lot, and immediately dive into another as the fox did.

11 August 1853 ❦ T HERE ARE BERRIES which men do not use like choke berries—which here in Hubbards Swamp grow in great profusion & blacken the bushes. How much richer we feel for this unused abundance & superfluity. Nature would not appear so rich—the profusion so rich if we knew a use for everything—

12 August 1851 ❦ 1 ½ AM. F ULL MOON Arose and went to the river and bathed, stepping very carefully not to disturb the household and still carefully in the street not to disturb the neighbors. I did not walk naturally & freely till I had got over the wall. Then to Hubbards bridge at 2 AM— There was a whippoorwill in the road just beyond Godwins which flew up & lighted on the fence & kept alighting on the fence within a rod of me & circling round me with a slight squeak as if inquisitive about me. I do not remember what I observed or thought in coming hither. The traveller's whole employment is to calculate what cloud will obscure the moon and what she will triumph over— In the after midnight hours the traveller's sole companion is the moon— All his thoughts are centered in her She is waging continual war with the clouds in his behalf

13 August 1854 ❦ S OCIETY SEEMS to have invaded and overrun me— I have drank tea & coffee—& made my-self cheap and vulgar—my days have been all noon tide without sacred mornings & evenings. I desire to rise early henceforth—to associate with those whose influence is elevating—To have such dreams & waking thoughts that my diet may not be indifferent to me.

14 August 1854 ❦ I NOW STANDING on the shore see that in sailing or floating down a smooth stream at evening—it is an advantage to the fancy to be thus slightly separated from the land. It is to be slightly removed from the commonplace of earth. To float thus on the silver plated stream—is like embarking in a train of thought itself— You are surrounded by water which is full of reflections—& you see the earth at a distance which is very agreeable to the imagination.

15 August 1858 ❦ RAIN IN THE NIGHT and dog-day weather again, after two clear days. I do not like the name "dog-days." Can we not have a new name for this season? It is the season of mould and mildew, and foggy, muggy, often rainy weather.

16 August 1851 ❦ IT IS TRUE man can and does live by preying on other animals, but this is a miserable way of sustaining himself—and he will be regarded as a benefactor of his race—along with Prometheus & Christ—who shall teach men to live on a more innocent & wholesome diet. Is it not already acknowledged to be a reproach that man is a carnivorous animal?

17 August 1851 ❦ THAT IN EACH SEASON when some part of nature especially flourishes—then a corresponding part of me may not fail to flourish.

18 August 1853 ❦ WHAT MEANS this sense of lateness that so comes over one now—as if the rest of the year were down hill, & if we had not performed anything before—we should not now— The season of flowers or of promise may be said to be over & now is the season of fruits—but where is our fruit? The night of the year is approaching, what have we done with our talent? All nature prompts & reproves us— How early in the year it begins to be late. The sound of the crickets even in the spring makes our hearts beat with its aweful reproof—while it encourages with its seasonable warning. It matters not by how little we have fallen behind—it seems irretrievably late. The year is full of warnings of its shortness—as is life—

19 August 1851 ❦ THE SEASONS DO NOT CEASE a moment to revolve and therefore nature rests no longer at her culminating point than at any other. If you are not out at the right instant the summer may go by & you not see it. How much of the year is spring & fall—how little can be called summer!

20 August 1851 ❦ A TRAVELLER WHO LOOKS at things with an impartial eye may see what the oldest inhabitant has not observed.

21 August 1852 ❦ THE SOUND of the crickets gradually prevails more and more. I hear the year falling asleep.

22 August 1860 ❦ IT IS TRUE, as is said, that we have as good a right to make berries private property as to make grass and trees such; but what I chiefly regret is the, in effect, dog-in-the-manger result, for at the same time that we exclude mankind from gathering berries in our field, we exclude them from gathering health and happiness and inspiration and a hundred other far finer and nobler fruits than berries, which yet we shall not gather ourselves there, nor even carry to market. We strike only one more blow at a simple and wholesome relation to nature.

23 August 1853 ❦ LIVE IN EACH SEASON as it passes; breathe the air, drink the drink, taste the fruit, and resign yourself to the influences of each. Let them be your only diet drink and botanical medicines. In August live on berries, not dried meats and pemmican, as if you were on shipboard making your way through a waste ocean, or in a northern desert. Be blown on by all the winds. Open all your pores and bathe in all the tides of Nature, in all her streams and oceans, at all seasons.

24 August 1852 ❦ THE YEAR is but a succession of days & I see that I could assign some office to each day—which summed up would be the history of the year— Everything is done in season and there is no time to spare— The bird gets its brood hatched in season & is off. I looked into the nest where I saw a vireo feeding its young a few days ago—but it is empty—it is fledged & flown.

25 August 1852 ❦ DOES A MIND in sympathy with nature need a hygrometer?

26 August 1859 ❦ THAT FIRST FROST on the 17th was the first stroke of winter aiming at the scalp of summer. Like a stealthy and insidious aboriginal enemy, it made its assault just before daylight in some deep and far-away hollow and then silently withdrew. Few have seen the drooping plants, but the news of this stroke circulates rapidly through the village. Men communicate it with a tone of warning. The foe is gone by sunrise, but some fearful neighbors who have visited their potato and cranberry patches report this stroke. The implacable and irresistible foe to all this tender greenness is not far off, nor can we be sure, any month in the year, that some scout from his low camp may not strike down the tenderest of the children of summer.

27 August 1859 ❧ W HAT IS OFTEN called poverty, but which is a simpler and truer relation to nature, gives a peculiar relish to life, just as to be kept short gives us an appetite for food.

28 August 1859 ❧ A COOL DAY; wind northwest. Need a half-thick coat. Thus gradually we withdraw into winter quarters. It is a clear, flashing air, and the shorn fields now look bright and yellowish and cool, tinkled and twittered over by bobolinks, goldfinches, sparrows, etc. You feel the less inclined to bathing this weather, and bathe from principle, when boys, who bathe for fun, omit it.

29 August 1852 ❧ W E BOAST THAT WE BELONG to the 19th century—and are making the most rapid strides of any nation But consider how little this village does for its own culture— perchance a comparatively decent system of common schools— schools for infants only, as it were, but excepting the half starved lyceum in the winter—no school for ourselves. It is time that we had uncommon schools—that we did not leave off our educa-tion when we begin to be men.

30 August 1856 ❧ M ANY OF OUR DAYS should be spent, not in vain expectations and lying on our oars, but in carrying out deliberately and faithfully the hundred little purposes which every man's genius must have suggested to him. Let not your life be wholly without an object, though it be only to ascertain the flavor of a cranberry, for it will not be only the quality of an insignificant berry that you will have tasted, but the flavor of your life to that extent, and it will be such a sauce as no wealth can buy.

31 August 1852 ❧ IT IS PLEASANT to embark on a voyage—if only for a short river excursion—the boat to be your home for the day—especially if it is neat & dry—a sort of moving studio it becomes—you can carry so many things with you— It is almost as if you put oars out at your windows—& moved your house along.

SEPTEMBER

1 September 1859 ❦ Bᴏᴜɢʜᴛ ᴀ ᴘᴀɪʀ ᴏꜰ sʜᴏᴇs the other day, and, observing that as usual they were only wooden-pegged at the toes, I required the seller to put in an extra row of iron pegs there while I waited for them. So he called to his boy to bring those zinc pegs, but I insisted upon iron pegs and no zinc ones. He gave me considerable advice on the subject of shoes, but I suggested that even the wearer of shoes, of whom I was one, had an opportunity to learn some of their qualities.

2 September 1856 ❦ Mʏ ꜰᴀᴛʜᴇʀ asked John Legross if he took an interest in politics and did his duty to his country at this crisis. He said he did. He went into the wood-shed and read the newspaper Sundays. Such is the dawn of the literary taste, the first seed of literature that is planted in the new country. His grandson may be the author of a Bhagvat-Geeta.

3 September 1851 ❦ As ꜰᴏʀ ᴡᴀʟᴋɪɴɢ the inhabitants of large English towns are confined almost exclusively to their parks & to the high ways—the few foot-paths in their vicinities "are gradually vanishing" says Wilkinson "under the encroachments of the proprietors."

He proposes that the peoples right to them be asserted & defended—& that they be kept in a passable state at the public expense— "This" says he, "would be easily done by means of asphalt laid upon a good foundation" !!! So much for walking and the prospects of walking in the neighborhood of English large towns.

Think of a man—he may be a genius of some kind—being confined to a high way & a park for his world to range in— I should die from mere nervousness at the thought of such confinement. I should hesitate before I were born if those terms were revealed to me. Fenced in forever by those green barriers of fields—where gentlemen are seated! Can they be said to be inhabitants of this globe. Will they be content to inhabit heaven thus partially?

4 September 1841 ❧ A BOOK SHOULD BE SO TRUE as to be intimate and familiar to all men—as the sun to their faces. Such a word as is occasionally uttered to a companion in the woods in summer, and both are silent.

5 September 1851 ❧ BY THE QUALITY of a man's writing—by the elevation of its tone you may measure his self-respect.

6 September 1851 ❧ THE UNWRITTEN LAWS are the most stringent.

7 September 1851 ❧ I CANNOT *easily* buy a blank book to write thoughts in, they are all ruled for dollars & cents.

8 September 1859 ❧ I WENT TO THE STORE the other day to buy a bolt for our front door, for, as I told the storekeeper, the Governor was coming here. "Aye," said he, "and the Legislature too." "Then I will take two bolts," said I.

9 September 1858 ❧ A MAN SEES only what concerns him. A botanist absorbed in the pursuit of grasses does not distinguish the grandest pasture oaks. He as it were tramples down oaks unwittingly in his walk.

10 September 1860 🌿 A LMOST EVERY PLANT, however humble, has thus its day, and sooner or later becomes the characteristic feature of some part of the landscape or other.

11 September 1851 🌿 W E HAVE HAD NO RAIN for a week & yet the pitcher plants have water in them.— Are they ever quite dry? Are they not replenished by the dews always—& being shaded by the grass saved from evaporation? What wells for the birds!

12 September 1858 🌿 T HE CINNAMON FERN has begun to yellow and wither. How rich in its decay! *Sic transit gloria mundi!* Die like the leaves, which are most beautiful in their decay. Thus gradually and successively each plant lends its richest color to the general effect, and in the fittest place, and passes away. Amid the October woods we hear no funereal bell, but the scream of the jay.

13 September 1852 🌿 I MUST WALK MORE with free senses— It is as bad to *study* stars & clouds as flowers & stones— I must let my senses wander as my thoughts—my eyes see without looking. Carlyle said that how to observe was to look—but I say that it is rather to see—& the more you look the less you will observe— I have the habit of attention to such excess that my senses get no rest—but suffer from a constant strain. Be not preoccupied with looking. Go not to the object let it come to you.

When I have found myself ever looking down & confining my gaze to the flowers—I have thought it might be well to get into the habit of observing the clouds as a corrective— But ha! that study would be just as bad— What I need is not to look at all—but a true sauntering of the eye.

14 September 1856 ❦ THE GARDENER with all his assiduity does not raise such a variety, nor so many successive crops on the same space, as Nature in the very roadside ditches.

15 September 1860 ❦ I LOVE TO SEE anything that implies a simpler mode of life and greater nearness to the earth.

16 September 1859 ❦ ASK ME FOR a certain number of dollars if you will, but do not ask me for my afternoons.

17 September 1839 ❦ NATURE never makes haste; her systems revolve at an even pace. The bud swells imperceptibly—without hurry or confusion, as though the short spring days were an eternity. All her operations seem separately for the time, the single object for which all things tarry.— Why then should man hasten as if any thing less than eternity were allotted for the least deed? Let him consume never so many aeons, so that he go about the meanest task well—though it be but the paring of his nails.

18 September 1859 ❦ DR. BARTLETT handed me a paper today, desiring me to subscribe for a statue to Horace Mann. I declined, and said that I thought a man ought not any more to take up room in the world after he was dead. We shall lose one advantage of a man's dying if we are to have a statue of him forthwith. This is probably meant to be an opposition statue to that of Webster. At this rate they will crowd the streets with them. A man will have to add a clause to his will, "No statue to be made of me." It is very offensive to my imagination to see the dying stiffen into statues at this rate. We should wait till their bones begin to crumble—and then avoid too near a likeness to the living.

19 September 1854 ❦ THINKING this afternoon of the prospect of my writing lectures and going abroad to read them the next winter, I realized how incomparably great the advantages of obscurity and poverty which I have enjoyed so long (and may still perhaps enjoy). I thought with what more than princely, with what poetical, leisure I had spent my years hitherto, without care or engagement, fancy-free. I have given myself up to nature; I have lived so many springs and summers and autumns and winters as if I had nothing else to do but *live* them, and imbibe whatever nutriment they had for me; I have spent a couple of years, for instance, with the flowers chiefly, having none other so binding engagement as to observe when they opened; I could have afforded to spend a whole fall observing the changing tints of the foliage. Ah, how I have thriven on solitude and poverty! I cannot overstate this advantage. I do not see how I could have enjoyed it, if the public had been expecting as much of me as there is danger now that they will. If I go abroad lecturing, how shall I ever recover the lost winter?

20 September 1852 ❦ THE SURFACE is not *perfectly* smooth, on account of the zephyr—& the reflections of the woods are a little indistinct and blurred. How soothing to sit on a stump on this height overlooking the pond and study the dimpling circles which are incessantly inscribed and again erased on the smooth and otherwise invisible surface, amid the reflected skies. The reflected sky is of a deeper blue How beautiful that over this vast expanse there can be no disturbance, but it is thus at once gently smoothed away & assuaged. as when a vase of water is jarred the trembling circles seek the shore & all is smooth again. Not a fish can leap or an insect fall on it but it is reported in lines of beauty—in circling dimples—as it were the constant welling up of its fountain—the gentle pulsing of its life—the heaving of its breast.

21 September 1852 ❦ How BEAUTIFUL when a whole maple on the edge of a swamp is like one great scarlet fruit—full of ripe juices— A sign of the ripening—every leaf from lowest limb to topmost spire—is a-glow.

22 September 1852 ❦ IN LOVE WE IMPART each to each—in subtlest immaterial form of thought or atmosphere the best of ourselves—such as commonly vanishes or evaporates in aspirations—& mutually enrich each other—

23 September 1859 ❦ SO LIVE THAT only the most beautiful wild-flowers will spring up where you have dwelt,—harebells, violets and blue-eyed grass.

24 September 1859 ❦ A MAN MUST ATTEND to Nature closely for many years to know when, as well as where, to look for his objects, since he must always anticipate her a little. Young men have not learned the phases of Nature; they do not know what constitutes a year, or that one year is like another. I would know when in the year to expect certain thoughts and moods, as the sportsman knows when to look for plover.

25 September 1851 ❦ SOME MEN ARE EXCITED by the smell of burning powder—but I thought in my dream last night how much saner to be excited by the smell of new bread.

26 September 1859 ❧ NATURE not only produces good wares, but puts them up handsomely. Witness these pretty-colored and variously shaped skins in which her harvests, the seeds of her various plants, are now being packed away. I know in what bags she puts her nightshade seeds, her cranberries, viburnums, cornels, by their form and color, often by their fragrance; and thus a legion of consumers find them.

27 September 1857 ❧ A SMALL RED MAPLE has grown, perchance, far away on some moist hillside, a mile from any road, unobserved. It has faithfully discharged the duties of a maple there, all winter and summer, neglected none of its economies, added to its stature in the virtue which belongs to a maple, by a steady growth all summer, and is nearer heaven than in the spring, never having gone gadding abroad; and now, in this month of September, when men are turned travellers, hastening to the seaside, or the mountains, or the lakes,—in this month of traveling,—this modest maple, having ripened its seeds, still without budging an inch, travels on its reputation, runs up its scarlet flag on that hillside, to show that it has finished its summer work before all other trees, and withdraws from the contest.

28 September 1859 ❧ IN PROPORTION as a man has a poor ear for music, or loses his ear for it, he is obliged to go far for it or fetch it from far, and pay a great price for such as he *can* hear. Operas, ballet-singers, and the like only affect him. It is like the difference between a young and healthy appetite and the appetite of an epicure, between a sweet crust and a mock-turtle soup.

29 September 1843 ❧ LET THE DESPARING RACE of men know that there is in Nature no sign of decay—but universal uninterrupted vigor— All waste and ruin has a speedy period. Who ever detected a wrinkle on her brow—or a weather seam—or a grey hair on her crown or a rent in her garment.

30 September 1851 ❧ IT IS WITH LEAVES as with fruits & woods—& animals & men—when they are mature their different characters appear.

OCTOBER

1 October 1851 ❦ 5 Pᴍ Jᴜsᴛ ᴘᴜᴛ a fugitive slave who has
taken the name of Henry Williams into the cars for Canada. He
escaped from Stafford County Virginia to Boston last October,
has been in Shadracks place at the Cornhill Coffee-house—had
been corresponding through an agent with his master who is
his father about buying—himself—his master asking $600 but
he having been able to raise only $500.— heard that there were
writs out for two Williamses fugitives—and was informed by
his fellow servants & employer that Augerhole Burns & others of
the police had called for him when he was out. Accordingly fled
to Concord last night on foot—bringing a letter to our family
from Mr Lovejoy of Cambridge—& another which Garrison
had formerly given him on another occasion.

He lodged with us & waited in the house till funds were collected with which to forward him. Intended to despatch him at
noon through to Burlington—but when I went to buy his ticket
saw one at the Depot who looked & behaved so much like a
Boston policeman, that I did not venture that time.

An intelligent and very well-behaved man, a mullatto.

2 October 1858 ❦ Tʜᴇ ᴄᴀᴛ ᴄᴏᴍᴇs ɪɴ from an early walk amid
the weeds. She is full of sparrows and wants no more breakfast
this morning, unless it be a saucer of milk, the dear creature. I
saw her studying ornithology between the corn-rows.

3 October 1859 ❦ LOOKING FROM the hog-pasture over the valley of Spencer Brook westward, we see the smoke rising from a huge chimney above a gray roof amid the woods, at a distance, where some family is preparing its evening meal. There are few more agreeable sights than this to the pedestrian traveller. No cloud is fairer to him than that little bluish one which issues from the chimney. It suggests all of domestic felicity beneath. There beneath, we suppose, that life is lived of which we have only dreamed. In our minds we clothe each unseen inhabitant with all the success, with all the serenity, which we can conceive of. If old, we imagine him serene; if young, hopeful. Nothing can exceed the perfect peace which reigns there. We have only to see a gray roof with its plume of smoke curling up amid the trees to have this faith. There we suspect no coarse haste or bustle, but serene labors which proceed at the same pace with the declining day. *There* is no hireling in the barn nor in the kitchen. Why does any distant prospect ever charm us? Because we instantly and inevitably imagine a life to be lived there such as is not lived elsewhere, or where we are. We presume that success is the rule. We forever carry a perfect sampler in our minds. Why are distant valleys, why lakes, why mountains in the horizon, ever fair to us? Because we realize for a moment that they may be the home of man, and that man's life may be in harmony with them. Shall I say that we thus forever delude ourselves?

4 October 1859 ❦ IT IS ONLY when we forget all our learning that we begin to know. I do not get nearer by a hair's breadth to any natural object so long as I presume that I have an introduction to it from some learned man. To conceive of it with a total apprehension I must for the thousandth time approach it as something totally strange. If you would make acquaintance with the ferns you must forget your botany. You must get rid of what is commonly called *knowledge* of them. Not a single scientific term or distinction is the least to the purpose, for you would fain perceive something, and you must approach the object totally unprejudiced. You must be aware that *no thing* is what you have taken it to be.

5 October 1856 ❦ IT IS WELL TO FIND your employment and amusement in simple and homely things. These wear best and yield most. I think I would rather watch the motions of these cows in their pasture for a day, which I now see all headed one way and slowly advancing,—watch them and project their course carefully on a chart, and report all their behavior faithfully,—than wander to Europe or Asia and watch other motions there; for it is only ourselves that we report in either case, and perchance we shall report a more restless and worthless self in the latter case than in the first.

6 October 1851 ❦ AS WE PADDLED DOWN the stream with our backs to the moon, we saw the reflection-of every wood & hill on both sides distinctly These answering reflections—shadow to substance,—impress the voyager with a sense of harmony & symmetry—as when you fold a blotted paper & produce a regular figure.— a dualism which nature loves. What you commonly see is but half.

7 October 1857 ❦ Nᴀᴛᴜʀᴇ ʜᴏʟᴅꜱ her annual fair and gala-days in October in every hollow and on every hillside.

Look into that hollow all aglow, where the trees are clothed in their vestures of most dazzling tints. Does it not suggest a thousand gypsies beneath, rows of booths, and that man's spirits should rise as high, that the routine of his life should be interrupted by an analogous festivity and rejoicing?

8 October 1851 ❦ Bʏ ᴛʜᴇ ꜱɪᴅᴇ of J. P. Browns grain field I picked up some white-oak acorns in the path by the woodside— which I found to be unexpectedly sweet & palateable, the bitterness being scarcely perceptible— To my taste they are quite as good as chestnuts. No wonder the first men lived on acorns Such as these are no mean food—such as they are represented to be. Their sweetness is like the sweetness of bread—and to have discovered this palatableness in this neglected nut—the whole world is to me the sweeter for it. I am related again to the first men. What can be handsomer—wear better to the eye—than the color of the acorn like the leaves on which they fall—polished. or varnished.

To find that acorns are edible—it is a greater addition to ones stock of life than would be imagined. I should be at least equally pleased if I were to find that the grass tasted sweet and nutritious— It increases the number of my friends—it diminishes the number of my foes. How easily at this season I could feed myself in the woods! There is mast for me too—as well as for the pigeon—& the squirrel.

9 October 1860 ❦ Tʜɪꜱ ʜᴀꜱᴛᴇ ᴛᴏ ᴋɪʟʟ a bird or quadruped and make a skeleton of it, which many young men and some old ones exhibit, reminds me of the fable of the man who killed the hen that laid golden eggs, and so got no more gold. It is a perfectly parallel case. Such is the knowledge which you may get from the anatomy as compared with the knowledge you get from the living creature.

10 October 1860 🌸 WENT TO A FIRE—or smoke—at Mrs. Hoar's. There is a slight blaze and more smoke. Two or three hundred men rush to the house, cut large holes in the roof, throw many hogsheads of water into it,—when a few pails full well directed would suffice,—and then they run off again, leaving your attic three inches deep with water, which is rapidly descending through the ceiling to the basement and spoiling all that can be spoiled, while a torrent is running down the stairways. They were very forward to put out the (fire), but they take no pains to put out the water, which does far more damage. The first was amusement; the last would be mere work and utility.

11 October 1840 🌸 THE TRUE MAN OF SCIENCE will have a rare Indian wisdom—and will know nature better by his finer organization. He will smell, taste, see, hear, feel, better than other men.

12 October 1858 🌸 I HAVE HEARD of judges, accidentally met at an evening party, discussing the efficacy of the laws and courts, and deciding that, with the aid of the jury system, "substantial justice was done." But taking those cases in which honest men refrain from going to law, together with those in which men, honest and dishonest, do go to law, I think that the law is really a "humbug," and a benefit principally to the lawyers. This town has made a law recently against cattle going at large, and assigned a penalty of five dollars. I am troubled by an Irish neighbor's cow and horse, and have threatened to have them put in the pound. But a lawyer tells me that these town laws are hard to put through, there are so many quibbles. He never knew the complainant to get his case if the defendant were a-mind to contend.

13 October 1859 ❦ THE SHAD-BUSH is leafing again by the sunny swamp-side. It is like a youthful or poetic thought in old age. Several times I have been cheered by this sight when surveying in former years. The chickadee seems to lisp a sweeter note at the sight of it. *I* would not fear the winter more than the shad-bush which puts forth fresh and tender leaves on its approach. In the fall I will take this for my coat-of-arms. It seems to detain the sun that expands it. These twigs are so full of life that they can hardly contain themselves. They ignore winter. They anticipate spring. What faith! Away in some warm and sheltered recess in the swamp you find where these leaves have expanded. It is a foretaste of spring. In my latter years, let me have some *shad-bush* thoughts.

14 October 1857 ❦ IT IS INDEED a golden autumn. These ten days are enough to make the reputation of any climate. A tradition of these days might be handed down to posterity. They deserve a notice in history, in the history of Concord. All kinds of crudities have a chance to get ripe this year. Was there ever such an autumn? And yet there was never such a panic and hard times in the commercial world. The merchants and banks are suspending and failing all the country over, but not the sandbanks, solid and warm, and streaked with bloody blackberry vines. You may run upon them as much as you please,—even as the crickets do, and find their account in it.

15 October 1859 ❧ EACH TOWN should have a park, or rather a primitive forest, of five hundred or a thousand acres, where a stick should never be cut for fuel, a common possession forever, for instruction and recreation. We hear of cow-commons and ministerial lots, but we want *men*-commons and lay lots, inalienable forever. Let us keep the New World *new*, preserve all the advantages of living in the country. There is meadow and pasture and wood-lot for the town's poor. Why not a forest and huckleberry-field for the town's rich? All Walden Wood might have been preserved for our park forever, with Walden in its midst, and the Easterbrooks Country, an unoccupied area of some four square miles, might have been our huckleberry field. If any owners of these tracts are about to leave the world without natural heirs who need or deserve to be specially remembered, they will do wisely to abandon their possession to all, and not will them to some individual who perhaps has enough already. As some give to Harvard College or another institution, why might not another give a forest or huckleberry field to Concord? A town is an institution which deserves to be remembered. We boast of our system of education, but why stop at schoolmasters and schoolhouses? We are all schoolmasters, and our schoolhouse is the universe. To attend chiefly to the desk or schoolhouse while we neglect the scenery in which it is placed is absurd. If we do not look out we shall find our fine schoolhouse standing in a cow-yard at last.

16 October 1859 ❧ MEN ATTACH a false importance to celestial phenomena as compared with terrestrial, as if it were more respectable and elevating to watch your neighbors than to mind your own affairs.

17 October 1859 ❦ WHEN LA MOUNTAIN and Haddock dropped down in the Canada wilderness the other day, they came near starving, or dying of cold and wet and fatigue, not knowing where to look for food nor how to shelter themselves. Thus far we have wandered from a simple and independent life. I think that a wise and independent, self-reliant man will have a complete list of the edibles to be found in a primitive country or wilderness, a bill of fare, in his waistcoat pocket at least, to say nothing of matches and warm clothing, so that he can commence a systematic search for them without loss of time. They might have had several frogs apiece if they had known how to find them. Talk about tariffs and protection of home industry, so as to be prepared for wars and hard times!! Here we are, deriving our breadstuffs from the West, our butter stuffs from Vermont, and our tea and coffee and sugar stuffs, and much more with which we stuff ourselves, from the other side of the globe. Why, a truly prudent man will carry such a list as the above, in his mind at least, even though he walk through Broadway or Quincy Market. He will know what are the permanent resources of the land and be prepared for the hardest of times.

18 October 1858 ❦ NO ANNUAL TRAINING or muster of soldiery, no celebration with its scarfs and banners, could import into the town a hundredth part of the annual splendor of our October. We have only to set the trees, or let them stand, and Nature will find the colored drapery,—flags of all her nations, some of whose private signals hardly the botanist can read. Let us have a good many maples and hickories and scarlet oaks, then, I say. Blaze away! Shall that dirty roll of bunting in the gunhouse be all the colors a village can display? A village is not complete unless it has these trees to mark the season in it. They are as important as a town clock.

19 October 1855 ❧ TALKING WITH BELLEW this evening about Fourierism and communities, I said that I suspected any enterprise in which two were engaged together. "But," said he, "it is difficult to make a stick stand unless you slant two or more against it." "Oh, no," answered I, "you may split its lower end into three, or drive it single into the ground, which is the best way; but most men, when they start out on a new enterprise, not only figuratively, but really, *pull up stakes.* When the sticks prop one another, none, or only one, stands erect."

20 October 1855 ❧ I HAVE COLLECTED and split up now quite a pile of driftwood,—rails and riders and stems and stumps of trees,—perhaps half or three-quarters of a tree. It is more amusing, not only to collect this with my boat and bring (it) up from the river on my back, but to split it also, than it would be to speak to a farmer for a load of wood and to saw and split that. Each stick I deal with has a history, and I read it as I am handling it, and, last of all, I remember my adventures in getting it, while it is burning in the winter evening. That is the most interesting part of its history.

21 October 1857 ❧ IS NOT THE POET bound to write his own biography? Is there any other work for him but a good journal? We do not wish to know how his imaginary hero, but how he, the actual hero, lived from day to day.

22 October 1859 ❧ JUST AS WE ARE doing away with duelling or fighting one another with pistols, I think that we may in course of time do away with fighting one another with lawyers. Such improvements are not altogether unheard of.

23 October 1855 ❦ Now is the time for chestnuts. A stone cast against the trees shakes them down in showers upon one's head and shoulders. But I cannot excuse myself for using the stone. It is not innocent, it is not just, so to maltreat the tree that feeds us. I am not disturbed by considering that if I thus shorten its life I shall not enjoy its fruit so long, but am prompted to a more innocent course by motives purely of humanity. I sympathize with the tree, yet I heaved a big stone against the trunks like a robber,—not too good to commit murder. I trust that I shall never do it again. These gifts should be accepted, not merely with gentleness, but with a certain humble gratitude. The tree whose fruit we would obtain should not be too rudely shaken even. It is not a time of distress, when a little haste and violence even might be pardoned. It is worse than boorish, it is criminal, to inflict an unnecessary injury on the tree that feeds or shadows us.

24 October 1857 ❦ I find my account in this long-continued monotonous labor of picking chestnuts all the afternoon, brushing the leaves aside without looking up, absorbed in that, and forgetting better things awhile. My eye is educated to discover anything on the ground, as chestnuts, etc. It is probably wholesomer to look at the ground much than at the heavens. As I go stooping and brushing the leaves aside by the hour, I am not thinking of chestnuts merely, but I find myself humming a thought of more significance. This occupation affords a certain broad pause and opportunity to start again afterward,—turn over a new leaf.

25 October 1852 ❧ THE AUTUMNAL TINTS grow gradually darker & duller— They are doing to a crisp. but not less rich to my eye— And now a hill side near the river exhibits the darkest crispy reds and browns of every hue all agreeably blended— At the foot next the meadow stands a front rank of smoke like maples bare of leaves—intermixed with yellow birches. Higher up red oaks of various shades of dull red—with yellowish perhaps black oaks intermixed—and walnuts now brown—& near the hill top or rising above the rest perhaps a still yellowed oak—& here and there amid the rest or in the fore ground on the meadow—dull ashy salmon-colored white oaks large & small—all these contrasting with the clear liquid sempiternal green of pines.

26 October 1853 ❧ WHEN, AFTER FEELING dissatisfied with my life, I aspire to something better, am more scrupulous, more reserved and continent, as if expecting somewhat, suddenly I find myself full of life as a nut of meat,—am overflowing with a quiet, genial mirthfulness. I think to myself, I must attend to my diet; I must get up earlier and take a morning walk; I must have done with luxuries and devote myself to my muse. So I dam up my stream, and my waters gather to a head. I am freighted with thought.

27 October 1855 ❧ THE OUTDOOR AIR and exercise which the walker gets give a different tone to his palate, and he craves a fruit which the sedentary would call harsh and crabbed even. The palate rejects a wild apple eaten in the house—so of haws and acorns—and demands a tamed one, for here you miss that October air which is the wine it is eaten with. I frequently pluck wild apples of so rich and spicy a flavor that I wonder all orchardists do not get a scion from them, but when I have brought home my pockets full, and taste them in the house, they are unexpectedly harsh, crude things. They must be eaten in the fields, when your system is all aglow with exercise, the frosty weather nips your fingers (in November), the wind rattles the bare boughs and rustles the leaves, and the jay is heard screaming around.

So there is one thought for the field, another for the house. I would have my thoughts, like wild apples, to be food for walkers, and will not warrant them to be palatable if tasted in the house.

28 October 1853 ❧ FOR A YEAR OR TWO PAST, my *publisher*, falsely so called, has been writing from time to time to ask what disposition should be made of the copies of "A Week on the Concord and Merrimack Rivers" still on hand, and at last suggesting that he had use for the room they occupied in his cellar. So I had them all sent to me here, and they have arrived to-day by express, filling the man's wagon,—706 copies out of an edition of 1000. . . . I have now a library of nearly nine hundred volumes, over seven hundred of which I wrote myself. Is it not well that the author should behold the fruits of his labor?

29 October 1858 ❧ NATURE NOW, like an athlete, begins to strip herself in earnest for her contest with her great antagonist Winter. In the bare trees and twigs what a display of muscle!

30 October 1853 ❧ WHAT WITH THE RAINS and frosts and winds, the leaves have fairly fallen now. You may say the fall has ended. Those which still hang on the trees are withered and dry. I am surprised at the change since last Sunday. Looking at the distant woods, I perceive that there is no yellow nor scarlet there now. They are (except the evergreens) a mere dull, dry red. The autumnal tints are gone. What life remains is merely at the foot of the leaf-stalk. The woods have for the most part acquired their winter aspect, and coarse, rustling, light-colored withered grasses skirt the river and the wood-side. This is November. The landscape prepared for winter, without snow. When the forest and fields put on their sober winter hue, we begin to look more to the sunset for color and variety.

October 31, 1858 ❦ AFTER WALKING for a couple of hours the other day through the woods, I came to the base of a tall aspen, which I do not remember to have seen before, standing in the midst of the woods in the next town, still thickly leaved and turned to greenish yellow. It is perhaps the largest of its species that I know. It was by merest accident that I stumbled on it, and if I had been sent to find it, I should have thought it to be, as we say, like looking for a needle in a haymow. All summer, and it chances for so many years, it has been concealed to me; but now, walking in a different direction, to the same hilltop from which I saw the scarlet oaks, and looking off just before sunset, when all other trees visible for miles around are reddish or green, I distinguish my new acquaintance by its yellow color. Such is its fame, at last, and reward for living in that solitude and obscurity. It is the most distinct tree in all the landscape, and would be the cynosure of all eyes here. Thus it plays its part in the choir.

1 November 1858 ❦ As the afternoons grow shorter, and the early evening drives us home to complete our chores, we are reminded of the shortness of life, and become more pensive, at least in this twilight of the year. We are prompted to make haste and finish our work before the night comes.

2 November 1858 ❦ The beauty of the earth answers exactly to your demand and appreciation.

3 November 1857 ❦ To see a remote landscape between two near rocks! I want no other gilding to my picture-frame. There they lie, as perchance they tumbled and split from off an iceberg. What better frame could you have? The globe itself, here named pasture, for ground and foreground, two great boulders for the sides of the frame, and the sky itself for the top! And for artists and subject, God and Nature! Such pictures cost nothing but eyes, and it will not bankrupt one to own them. They were not stolen by any conqueror as spoils of war, and none can doubt but they are really the works of an old master.

4 November 1840 ❦ By your few words show how insufficient would be many words.

5 November 1855 ❦ I know many children to whom I would fain make a present on some one of their birthdays, but they are so far gone in the luxury of presents—have such perfect museums of costly ones—that it would absorb my entire earnings for a year to buy them something which would not be beneath their notice.

6 November 1853 ❧ How much handsomer a river or lake such as ours, seen thus through a foreground of scattered or else partially leafless trees, though at a considerable distance this side of it, especially if the water is open, without wooded shores or isles! It is the most perfect and beautiful of all frames, which yet the sketcher is commonly careful to brush aside. I mean a pretty thick foreground, a view of the distant water through the near forest, through a thousand little vistas, as we are rushing toward the former,—that intimate mingling of wood and water which excites an expectation which the near and open view rarely realizes.

7 November 1858 ❧ The very earth is like a house shut up for the winter, and I go knocking about it in vain. But just then I heard a chickadee on a hemlock, and was inexpressibly cheered to find that an old acquaintance was yet stirring about the premises, and was, I was assured, to be there all winter. All that is evergreen in me revived at once.

8 November 1853 ❧ Birds generally wear the russet dress of nature at this season. They have their fall no less than the plants; the bright tints depart from their foliage or feathers, and they flit past like withered leaves in rustling flocks.

9 November 1855 ❧ FOUND A GOOD STONE JUG, small size, float-ing stopple up. I drew the stopple and smelled, as I expected, molasses and water, or something stronger (black-strap?), which it *had* contained. Probably some meadow haymakers' jug left in the grass, which the recent rise of the river has floated off. It will do to put with the white pitcher I found and keep flowers in. Thus I get my furniture.

10 November 1851 ❧ POLITICS IS, as it were, the gizzard of society—full of grit & gravel and the two political parties are its two opposite halves—which grind on each other. Not only individuals but states have thus a confirmed dispepsia—which expresses itself—you can imagine by what sort of eloquence.

11 November 1858 ❧ THE SCARLET OAK LEAF! What a grace-ful and pleasing outline! a combination of graceful curves and angles. These deep bays in the leaf are agreeable to us as the thought of deep and secure havens to the mariner. But both your love of repose and your spirit of adventure are addressed, for both bays and headlands are represented,—sharp-pointed rocky capes and rounded bays with smooth strands. To the sailor's eye it is a much indented shore, and in his casual glance he thinks that if he doubles its sharp capes he will find a haven in its deep rounded bays. If I were a drawing master, I would set my pupils to copying these leaves, that they might learn to draw firmly and gracefully. It is a shore to the aerial ocean, on which the windy surf beats. How different from the white oak leaf with its rounded headlands, on which no lighthouse need be placed!

12 November 1853 ❦ I CANNOT BUT REGARD it as a kindness in those who have the steering of me that, by the want of pecuniary wealth, I have been nailed down to this my native region so long and steadily, and made to study and love this spot of earth more and more. What would signify in comparison a thin and diffused love and knowledge of the whole earth instead, got by wandering? The traveller's is but a barren and comfortless condition. Wealth will not buy a man a home in nature,—house nor farm there. The man of business does not by his business earn a residence in nature, but is denaturalized rather. What is a farm, house and land, office or shop, but a settlement in nature under the most favorable conditions? It is insignificant, and a merely negative good fortune, to be provided with thick garments against cold and wet, an unprofitable, weak and defensive condition, compared with being able to extract some exhilaration, some warmth even, out of cold and wet themselves, and to clothe them with our sympathy. The rich man buys woollens and furs, and sits naked and shivering still in spirit, besieged by cold and wet. But the poor Lord of Creation, cold and wet he makes to warm him, and be his garments.

13 November 1857 ❦ SEE THE SUN RISE OR SET if possible each day. Let that be your pill.

14 November 1853 ❦ OCTOBER ANSWERS to that period in the life of man when he is no longer dependent on his transient moods, when all his experience ripens into wisdom, but every root, branch, leaf of him glows with maturity. What he has been and done in his spring and summer appears. He bears fruit.

15 November 1853 ❦ AFTER HAVING some business dealings with men, I am occasionally chagrined, and feel as if I had done some wrong, and it is hard to forget the ugly circumstance. I see that such intercourse long continued would make one thoroughly prosaic, hard, and coarse. But the longest intercourse with Nature, though in her rudest moods, does not thus harden and make coarse. A hard, insensible man whom we liken to a rock is indeed much harder than a rock. From hard, coarse, insensible men with whom I have no sympathy, I go to commune with the rocks, whose hearts are comparatively soft.

16 November 1851 ❦ THINKERS & WRITERS are in foolish haste to come before the world—with crude works. Young men are persuaded by their friends or by their own restless ambition, to write a course of lectures in a summer against the ensuing winter— And what it took the lecturer a summer to write it will take his audience but an hour to forget. If time is short— then you have no time to waste.

17 November 1850 ❦ THE NEWSPAPERS are the ruling power What Congress does is an after-clap.

18 November 1857 ❦ I HAD YESTERDAY a kink in my back and a general cold, and as usual it amounted to a cessation of life. I lost for the time my *rapport* or relation to nature. Sympathy with nature is an evidence of perfect health. You cannot perceive beauty but with a serene mind.

19 November 1853 ❦ WHAT IS THE PECULIARITY of the Indian summer? From the 14th to the 21st October inclusive, this year, was perfect Indian summer; and this day the next? Methinks that any particularly pleasant and warmer weather after the middle of October is thus called. Has it not fine, calm spring days answering to it?

20 November 1851 ❦ IT IS OFTEN SAID that melody can be heard farther than noise—& the finest melody farther than the coarsest. I think there is truth in this—& that accordingly those strains of the piano which reach me here in my attic stir me so much more than the sounds which I should hear if I were below in the parlor—because they are so much purer & diviner melody. They who sit farthest off from the noisy & bustling world are not at pains to distinguish what is sweet & musical—for that alone can reach them.

21 November 1860 ❦ ANOTHER FINGER-COLD EVENING, which I improve in pulling my turnips—the usual amusement of such weather—before they shall be frozen in. It is worth the while to see how green and lusty they are yet, still adding to their stock of nutriment for another year; and between the green and also withering leaves it does me good to see their great crimson round or scalloped tops, sometimes quite above ground, they are so bold. They remind you of rosy cheeks in cool weather, and indeed there is a relationship. All kinds of harvesty, even pulling turnips when the first cold weather numbs your fingers, are interesting, if you have been the sower, and have not sown too many.

22 November 1860 ❦ SIMPLY TO SEE to a distant horizon through a clear air,—the fine outline of a distant hill or a blue mountain-top through some new vista,—this is wealth enough for one afternoon.

23 November 1852 ❦ THERE IS SOMETHING GENIAL even in the first snow—& nature seems to relent a little of her November harshness. Men too are disposed to give thanks for the bounties of the year all over the land—& the sound of the mortar is heard in all houses—& the odor of summer savory reaches even to poets' garrets.

24 November 1857 ❦ SOME POETS have said that writing poetry was for youths only, but not so. In that fervid and excitable season we only get the impulse which is to carry us onward in our future career. Ideals are then exhibited to us distinctly which all our lives after we may aim at but not attain.

25 November 1858 ❦ WHILE MOST KEEP CLOSE to their parlor fires this cold and blustering Thanksgiving afternoon, and think with compassion of those who are abroad, I find the sunny south side of this swamp as warm as their parlors, and warmer to my spirit. Aye, there is a serenity and warmth here which the parlor does not suggest, enhanced by the sound of the wind roaring on the northwest side of the swamp a dozen or so rods off.

26 November 1860 ❦ A MAN FITS OUT A SHIP at a great expense and sends it to the West Indies with a crew of men and boys, and after six months or a year it comes back with a load of pineapples. Now, if no more gets accomplished than the speculator commonly aims at,—if it simply turns out what is called a successful venture,—I am less interested in this expedition than in some child's first excursion a-huckleberrying, in which it is introduced into a new world, experiences a new development, though it brings home only a gill of huckleberries in its basket. I know that the newspapers and the politicians declare otherwise, but they do not alter the fact. Then, I think that the fruit of the latter expedition was finer than that of the former. It was a more fruitful expedition. The value of any experience is measured, of course, not by the amount of money, but the amount of development we get out of it. If a New England boy's dealings with oranges and pineapples have had more to do with his development than picking huckleberries or pulling turnips have, then he rightly and naturally thinks more of the former; otherwise not.

Do not think that the fruits of New England are mean and insignificant, while those of some foreign land are noble and memorable. Our own, whatever they may be, are far more important to us than any others can be. They educate us, and fit us to live in New England. Better for us is the wild strawberry than the pineapple, the wild apple than the orange, the hazelnut or pignut than the cocoanut or almond, and not on account of their flavor merely, but the part they play in our education.

27 November 1857 ❦ STANDING BEFORE Stacy's large glass windows this morning, I saw that they were gloriously ground by the frost. I never saw such beautiful feather and fir-like frosting. His windows are filled with fancy articles and toys for Christmas and New-Year's presents, but this delicate and graceful outside frosting surpassed them all infinitely.

28 November 1859 ❦ THERE IS SCARCELY a wood of sufficient size and density left now for an owl to haunt in, and if I hear one hoot I may be sure where he is.

29 November 1858 ❧ How BRIGHT AND LIGHT the day now! Methinks it is as good as half an hour added to the day. White houses no longer stand out and stare in the landscape. The pine woods snowed up look more like the bare oak woods with their gray boughs. The river meadows show now far off a dull straw-color or pale brown amid the general white, where the coarse sedge rises above the snow; and distant oak woods are now more distinctly reddish. It is a clear and pleasant winter day. The snow has taken all the November out of the sky.

30 November 1853 ❧ A MAN ADVANCES in his walk somewhat as a river does, meanderingly, and such, too, is the progress of the race. The law that plants the rushes in waving lines along the edge of a pond, and that curves the pondshore itself, incessantly beats against the straight fences and highways of men and makes them conform to the line of beauty which is most agreeable to the eye at last.

DECEMBER

1 December 1856 ❧ SLATE-COLORED SNOWBIRDS flit before me in the path, feeding on the seeds on the snow, the countless little brown seeds that begin to be scattered over the snow, so much the more obvious to bird and beast. A hundred kinds of indigenous grain are harvested now, broadcast upon the surface of the snow. Thus at a critical season these seeds are shaken down on to a clean white napkin, unmixed with dirt and rubbish, and off this the little pensioners pick them. Their clean table is thus spread a few inches or feet above the ground.

2 December 1856 ❧ AS FOR THE SENSUALITY in Whitman's "Leaves of Grass," I do not so much wish that it was not written, as that men and women were so pure that they could read it without harm.

3 December 1855 ❧ EVERY LARGER TREE which I knew and admired is being gradually culled out and carried to mill. I see one or two more large oaks in E. Hubbard's wood lying high on stumps, waiting for snow to be removed. I miss them as surely and with the same feeling that I do the old inhabitants out of the village street. To me they were something more than timber; to their owner not so.

4 December 1856 ❧ I LOVE THE FEW homely colors of Nature at this season,—her strong wholesome browns, her sober and primeval grays, her celestial blue, her vivacious green, her pure, cold, snowy white.

5 December 1856 ❧ I LOVE THE WINTER, with its imprisonment and its cold, for it compels the prisoner to try new fields and resources. I love to have the river closed up for a season and a pause put to my boating, to be obliged to get my boat in. I shall launch it again in the spring with so much more pleasure. This is an advantage in point of abstinence and moderation compared with the seaside boating, where the boat ever lies on the shore. I love best to have each thing in its season only, and enjoy doing without it at all other times.

6 December 1859 ❧ THE BRIGHT-YELLOW sulphur lichens on the walls of the Walden road look novel, as if I had not seen them for a long time. Do they not require cold as much as moisture to enliven them? What surprising forms and colors! Designed on every natural surface of rock or tree. Even stones of smaller size which make the walls are so finished, and piled up for what use? How naturally they adorn our works of art! See where the farmer has set up his post-and-rail fences along the road. The sulphur lichen has, as it were, at once leaped to occupy the northern side of each post, as in towns handbills are pasted on all bare surfaces, and the rails are more or less gilded with them as if it had rained gilt.

7 December 1856 ❧ THE WINTERS COME now as fast as snowflakes. It is wonderful that old men do not lose their reckoning. It was summer, and now again it is winter. Nature loves this rhyme so well that she never tires of repeating it. So sweet and wholesome is the winter, so simple and moderate, so satisfactory and perfect, that her children will never weary of it.

8 December 1854 ❦ Winter has come unnoticed by me, I have been so busy writing. This is the life most lead in respect to Nature. How different from my habitual one! It is hasty, coarse, and trivial, as if you were a spindle in a factory. The other is leisurely, fine, and glorious, like a flower. In the first case you are merely getting your living; in the second you live as you go along.

9 December 1856 ❦ When I get as far as my bean-field, the reflected white in the winter horizon of this perfectly cloud-less sky is being condensed at the horizon's edge, and its hue deepening into a dun golden, against which the tops of the trees—pines and elms—are seen with beautiful distinctness, and a slight blush begins to suffuse the eastern horizon, and so the picture of the day is done and set in a gilded frame.

Such is a winter eve. Now for a merry fire, some old poet's pages, or else serene philosophy, or even a healthy book of trav-els, to last far into the night, eked out perhaps with the walnuts which we gathered in November.

10 December 1840 ❦ I discover a strange track in the snow, and learn that some migrating otter has made across from the river to the wood, by my yard and the smith's shop, in the silence of the night.— I cannot but smile at my own wealth, when I am thus reminded that every chink and cranny of nature is full to overflowing.— That each instant is crowded full of great events. Such an incident as this startles me with the assurance that the primeval nature is still working and makes tracks in the snow.

11 December 1855 ❦ From the right point of view, every storm and every drop in it is a rainbow.

12 December 1841 ❦ Who hears the rippling of the rivers will not utterly despair of anything.

13 December 1859 ❦ My first true winter walk is perhaps that which I take on the river, or where I cannot go in the summer. It is the walk peculiar to winter, and now first I take it. I see that the fox too has already taken the same walk before me, just along the edge of the buttonbushes, where not even he can go in the summer. We both turn our steps hither at the same time.

14 December 1851 ❦ As for the weather, all seasons are pretty much alike to one who is actively at work in the woods. I should say—that there were two or three remarkably warm days—& as many cold ones in the course of a year—but the rest are all alike—in respect to temperature— This is my answer to my acquaintances who ask me if I have not found it very cold being out all day.

15 December 1840 ❦ It is pleasant to work out of doors— My pen knife glitters in the sun—my voice is echoed from the woods, if an oar drops I am fain to drop it again, if my cane strikes a stone, I strike it again— Such are the accoustics of my work shop.

16 December 1840 ❦ Beauty is where it is perceived. When I see the sun shining on the woods across the pond, I think this side the richer which sees it.

17 December 1851 ❦ Improve every opportunity to express yourself in writing as if it were your last.

18 December 1841 ❧ SOME MEN MAKE their due impression upon their generation—because a petty occasion is enough to call forth all their energies—but are there not others who would rise to much heigher levels whom the world has never provoked to make the effort—I believe there are men now living who have never opened their mouths in a public assembly in whom nevertheless there is such a well of eloquence that the appetite of any age could never exhaust it.

19 December 1850 ❧ THE WILD-APPLES are frozen as hard as stones and rattle in my pockets but I find that they soon thaw when I get to my chamber & yieeld a sweet cider— I am astonished that the animals make no more use of them.

20 December 1851 ❧ BE FAITHFUL to your genius—write in the strain that interests you most- Consult not the popular taste.

21 December 1851 ❧ I AM OF THE NATURE of Stone. It takes the summer's sun to warm it.

22 December 1853 ❧ SURVEYING the last three days. They have not yielded much that I am aware of. All I find is old boundmarks, and the slowness and dullness of farmers reconfirmed. They even complain that I walk too fast for them. Their legs have become stiff from toil. This coarse and hurried outdoor work compels me to live grossly or be inattentive to my diet; that is the worst of it. Like work, like diet; that, I find, is the rule. Left to my chosen pursuits, I should never drink tea nor coffee, nor eat meat. The diet of any class or generation is the natural result of its employment and locality.

23 December 1851 ❦ It is a record of the mellow & ripe moments that I would keep.

I would not preserve the husk of life—but the kernel.

24 December 1841 ❦ I want to go soon and live away by the pond where I shall hear only the wind whispering among the reeds— It will be success if I shall have left myself behind, But my friends ask what I will do when I get there? Will it not be employment enough to watch the progress of the seasons?

25 December 1840 ❦ The character of Washington has after all been undervalued, simply because not valued correctly. He was a proper Puritan hero. It is his erectness and persistency which attract me. A few simple deeds with a dignified silence for background and that is all.

He never fluctuated, nor lingered, nor stooped, nor swerved, but was nobly silent and assured. He was not the darling of the people, as no man of integrity can ever be, but was as much respected as loved. His instructions to his steward—his refusal of a crown—his interview with his officers at the termination of the war,—his thoughts after his retirement as expressed in a letter to La Fayette—his remarks to another correspondent on his being chosen President—his last words to Congress—and the unparalleled respect which his most distinguished contemporaries—as Fox and Erskine, expressed for him—are refreshing to read in these unheroic days.

26 December 1860 ❦ To such a pass our civilization and division of labor has come that A, a professional huckleberry-picker, has hired B's field and, we will suppose, is now gathering the crop, perhaps with the aid of a patented machine; C, a professed cook, is superintending the cooking of a pudding made of some of the berries; while Professor D, for whom the pudding is intended, sits in his library writing a book,—a work on the Vaccinieae, of course. And now the result of this downward course will be seen in that book, which should be the ultimate fruit of the huckleberry field and account for the existence of the two professors who come between D and A. It will be worthless. There will be none of the spirit of the huckleberry in it. The reading of it will be a weariness to the flesh. To use a homely illustration, this is to save at the spile but waste at the bung. I believe in a different kind of division of labor, and that Professor D should divide himself between the library and the huckleberry-field.

27 December 1857 ❦ I AM DISAPPOINTED by most essays and lectures. I find that I had expected the authors would have some life, some very private experience, to report, which would make it comparatively unimportant in what style they expressed themselves, but commonly they have only a talent to exhibit. The new magazine which all have been expecting may contain only another love story as naturally told as the last, perchance, but without the slightest novelty in it.

28 December 1852 ❦ A BROAD MARGIN of leisure is as beautiful in a man's life as in a book. Haste makes waste no less in life than in housekeeping. Keep the time—observe the hours of the universe—not of the cars.

29 December 1858 ❦ I THINK MORE OF SKATES than of the horse or locomotive as annihilators of distance, for while I am getting along with the speed of the horse, I have at the same time the satisfaction of the horse and his rider, and far more adventure and variety than if I were riding. We never cease to be surprised when we observe how swiftly the skater glides along.

30 December 1853 ❦ IN WINTER even man is to a slight extent dormant, just as some animals are but partially awake, though not commonly classed with those that hibernate.

31 December 1859 ❦ HOW VAIN TO TRY to teach youth, or anybody, truths! They can only learn them after their own fashion, and when they get ready.

A NOTE ON TEXTS

For nearly a century the standard edition has been *The Writings of Henry David Thoreau*, edited by Bradford Torrey and Francis H. Allen, 20 volumes (Boston: Houghton Mifflin, 1906), volumes VII to XX of which comprise the *Journal* (separately numbered I to XIV). The 1906 Houghton Mifflin edition is being superseded by the ongoing *The Writings of Henry D. Thoreau* (Princeton, N.J.: Princeton University Press, 1971–), which among other titles has published seven volumes of the *Journal* to date. The Princeton edition of the *Journal* prints Thoreau's text exactly as it appears in manuscript and retains all peculiarities of his spelling, punctuation, and syntax. The Spirit of Thoreau series makes occasional editorial interpolations—indicated by square brackets—for cases in which the Princeton literal transcription might cause confusion and to provide context for certain passages.

FURTHER READING

Works by Thoreau

❧ *Cape Cod.* Edited by Joseph J. Moldenhauer. Princeton: Princeton University Press, 1988.

❧ *Collected Essays and Poems.* Selected by Elizabeth Hall Witherell. New York: Library of America, 2001.

❧ *The Correspondence of Henry David Thoreau.* Edited by Walter Harding and Carl Bode. New York: New York University Press, 1958. Reprint, Westport, Conn.: Greenwood, 1974.

❧ *Faith in a Seed: The Dispersion of Seeds and Other Late Natural History Writings.* Edited by Bradley P. Dean. Washington, D.C.: Island Press, 1993.

❧ *The Journal of Henry David Thoreau.* Volumes I–XIV. Edited by Bradford Torrey and Francis Allen. 1906. Reprint, Boston: Houghton Mifflin, 1949.

❧ *Journal.* Volumes 1–6, 8. Elizabeth Hall Witherell, editor-in-chief. Princeton: Princeton University Press, 1981–2002.

❧ *The Maine Woods.* Edited by Joseph J. Moldenhauer. Princeton: Princeton University Press, 1972.

❧ *Reform Papers.* Edited by Wendell Glick. Princeton: Princeton University Press, 1973.

❧ *Walden.* Edited by J. Lyndon Shanley. Princeton: Princeton University Press, 1971.

❧ *Walden.* Annotated edition edited by Jeffrey S. Cramer. New Haven: Yale University Press, 2004.

❧ *A Week on the Concord and Merrimack Rivers.* Edited by Carl F. Hovde, William Howarth, and Elizabeth Hall Witherell. Princeton: Princeton University Press, 1980.

Further Reading

Other Works

❦ Foster, David R. *Thoreau's Country: Journey through a Transformed Landscape.* Cambridge: Harvard University Press, 1999.

❦ Harding, Walter. *The Days of Henry Thoreau: A Biography.* Princeton: Princeton University Press, 1992.

❦ Richardson, Robert D., Jr. *Henry Thoreau: A Life of the Mind.* Berkeley and Los Angeles: University of California Press, 1986.

THE SPIRIT OF THOREAU

"How many a man has dated a new era in his life from the reading of a book," wrote Henry David Thoreau in *Walden*. Today that book, perhaps more than any other American work, continues to provoke, inspire, and change lives all over the world, and each rereading is fresh and challenging. Yet as Thoreau's countless admirers know, there is more to the man than *Walden*. An engineer, poet, teacher, naturalist, lecturer, and political activist, he truly had several more lives to lead, and each one speaks forcefully to us today.

The Spirit of Thoreau introduces the thoughts of a great writer on a variety of important topics, some that we readily associate him with, some that may be surprising. Each book includes selections from his familiar published works as well as from less well known and recently discovered lectures, letters, and journal entries. Thoreau claimed that "to read well, that is, to read true books in a true spirit, is a noble exercise, and one that will task the reader more than any exercise which the customs of the day esteem." The volume editors and the Thoreau Society believe that you will find these new aspects of Thoreau an exciting "exercise" indeed.

The Thoreau Society is honored to bring you these titles in cooperation with the University of Massachusetts Press. The publisher of many important studies of Thoreau and other Transcendentalists, the press is also widely recognized for its outstanding titles on several aspects of New England culture.

You are invited to continue exploring Thoreau by joining our society. For more than sixty years we have presented publications, annual gatherings, and other programs to further the appreciation of

The Spirit of Thoreau

Thoreau's thought and writings. In ways that the author of *Walden* could not have imagined, his message is still changing lives in a brand-new era.

For membership information, write to The Thoreau Society, 55 Old Bedford Road, Concord, Massachusetts 01742; call 978-369-5310; or visit our website www.thoreausociety.org.

WESLEY T. MOTT
Series Editor
The Thoreau Society

❦

STEVE GRANT
writes about nature and history
for the *Hartford Courant*.
He lives in Newtown,
Connecticut.